FIGHT BACK

A Woman's Guide to Self-defense that Works

Loren W. Christensen

and

Lisa Place

Turtle Press   **Santa Fe, NM**

To contact the author or to order additional copies of this book:
Turtle Press
PO Box 34010
Santa Fe NM 87594-4010
1-800-778-8785
www.TurtlePress.com

ISBN 978-1-934903-24-7
LCCN 2011003508

Printed in the United States of America

Warning-Disclaimer

This book is designed to provide information on the techniques and skills of self-defense It is not the purpose of this book to reprint all the information that is otherwise available to the author, publisher, printer or distributors, but instead to compliment, amplify and supplement other texts. You are urged to read all available material, learn as much as you wish about the subjects covered in this book and tailor the information to your individual needs. Anyone practicing the skills, exercises, drills or techniques presented in this book should be physically healthy enough to do so and have permission from a licensed physician before participating.

Every effort has been made to make this book as complete and accurate as possible. However, there may be mistakes, both typographical and in content. Therefore, this text should be used only as a general guide and not as the ultimate source of information on the subjects presented here in this book on any topic, skill or subject. The purpose of this book is to provide information and entertain. The authors, publisher, printer and distributors shall neither have liability nor responsibility to any person or entity with respect to loss or damages caused, or alleged to have been caused, directly or indirectly, by the information contained in this book. If you do not wish to be bound by the above, you may return this book to the publisher for a full refund.

Library of Congress Cataloging-in-Publication Data

Christensen, Loren W.

    Fight back : a woman's guide to self-defense that works / Loren W. Christensen and Lisa Place.
      p. cm.
    ISBN 978-1-934903-24-7
    1. Self-defense for women. I. Place, Lisa. II. Title.
    GV1111.5.C39 2011
    613.66082--dc22
                           2011003508

Acknowledgements

To our daughters: A'lyse Place, Amy Widmer and Carrie Christensen

We pray you never have to use the material in this book, but if you do, simply reach down past your societal graces, unleash that salivating lioness with you, and command her, "Get 'em!"

A BIG THANKS TO OUR PHOTOGRAPHERS:

Amy Widmer, A'lyse Place, David Tankersley, and Loren W. Christensen

AND TO OUR MODELS:

Rickie Place

A'lyse Place

Jace Widmer

Amy Widmer

Lisa Place

Loren W. Christensen

Self-defense in the News

One night in our city, Portland, Oregon, 51-year-old nurse Susan Kuhnhausen returned home after an evening working the emergency room in one of our hospitals. She had taken only a couple of steps into her dark house before an intruder, armed with a claw hammer, charged at her from a side room and smashed the tool into her skull. Incredibly, not only did she not lose consciousness, she began to fight the man who had been hired by her husband to kill her. They struggled in a furious battle all about the room and on the floor, punching and kicking each other in violent desperation. At one point, the nurse managed to take away the hammer from the hitman and slammed its steel head into his bones and tissue as he chewed on her flesh like a manic animal.

Mrs. Kuhnhausen, who outweighed the hitman by 80 pounds and had been fighting violent patients in the ER for years, fought her way behind the now frantic man, and wrapped her arm around his neck. He struggled with ferocity against her powerful hold but she continued constricting breath from his lungs and vital blood to his brain. With each passing second, he grew weaker and weaker until first his brain slipped into unconsciousness and then his heart ceased to beat.

Death by strangulation, the autopsy report would read.

During the trial, in which her husband would be sentenced to 10 years for his role in the attempted murder, Susan Kuhnhausen, who had taken the stand, leaned toward him, and said calmly, "If I ever, ever believed that you deserved to be dead, I would of at least had the balls to kill you myself."

Contents

Foreword by Gavin de Becker

Gavin de Becker is the best-selling author of *The Gift of Fear,* the most widely read self-defense book in the world. His books have been featured in *Time* and *Newsweek*, and many times on *The Oprah Winfrey Show*, including a special hour-long episode which commemorated the 10th anniversary of the publication of *The Gift of Fear*. His books are now published in fourteen languages. He can be contacted at www.gavindebecker.com.

The primary goal of this book is to teach people to survive a violent physical encounter. The exchange of energy between aggressor and defender cannot be fully appreciated from the comfort and distance of wherever you are reading these words. In actual attacks, events are absorbed through every sense, taken in via taste, smell, touch, and through the skin, literally. That's all the more reason we can benefit so much from having good information in advance.

Human beings aren't natural fighters; we didn't get the sharpest claws or strongest jaws or fastest legs. We got the biggest brains—and Loren Christensen and Lisa Place offer much-needed teaching on how the brain and body can work together toward the goal of prevailing in an attack. Loren has been a teacher of survival strategies since 1965, he's authored over 45 books and this one puts it all together for the audience that needs it most: Women.

Why do women need it most? Because women are victimized most often, and because our culture has prepared women least effectively. The culture has sold the (false) idea that survival is always more likely if you do what a predator tells you to do, if you submit. Women have been persuaded to believe that violence is a mystery that can be understood only by men.

Perhaps more than anything else offered in these pages is the gift of practicality and reality, ways to avoid offensive and unwanted advances and confrontations in everyday situations. This book details physical, non-verbal warning signs to help readers detect danger through behavioral cues. You'll learn skills used by warriors, and see that you too can be a warrior when you need to be. You'll see that you don't have to relinquish your control to a predator, that you can physically resist—even if you've spent years thinking you'd better not.

Trained for decades to interact with men in ways that serve the patriarchy, readers who fully absorb the information here can say No when they choose to. And I mean say No with muscles as well as words.

Safety starts with knowing that your intuition about people is a brilliant guardian. Listening to intuition really means listening to yourself. Like everyone, you've had scores of experiences when you listened and were later grateful, and scores of experiences when you chose not to listen, and were later regretful. I can't say it any more clearly than this: To protect yourself, you must believe in yourself. Nothing will encourage that belief more than knowing you are prepared.

Unlike many self-defense guides, and unlike advice given wholesale to girls and young women as they grow up, Loren Christensen and Lisa Place do not recommend submission when attacked. That option, of course, will always be available to those who feel in a given moment that it's the wisest course. But Loren and Lisa add many other options, many other weapons, including those he calls "weapons of opportunity" —and including the ones you're born with: elbows, knees, fingers, etc.

Too many women have been prepared for victimization through a lifetime of being warned that they ought to submit to violence or submit when even threatened. For women who have moved past that idea, who are willing to resist violence, this book can offer a new way of organizing your thinking on the subject: You can act defensively or offensively.

What I mean is that a woman who sees that violence is underway might have the thought "I have to defend myself now."

Another woman in the same situation might have the thought "He acted *offensively* so I am going to respond offensively—and in a manner that will not allow him to act again."

If you're a reader drawn to the second thought process, you're holding the right book—because here it all gets real practical real quick. There's information here about the physical aspects of predatory attack, and as important, the physical aspects of counter attack.

The topics of violence and self-defense aren't always pleasant, of course, so each person must ask herself: Do you want this information? If not, I pose an easier, softer question: Of all the approaches you might take to enhancing your safety, do you suppose that ignorance about violence is an effective one?

This book teaches that our primary defense weapons are the mind and the heart. The heart I'm referring to here isn't just the one that gives love and courage and perseverance; it's also the organ that pumps extra blood to the arms and legs, the organ that gives extra energy and strength to the muscles when needed. That's how practical and realistic the heart can be when it comes to our safety.

Somewhere in America right now are four or five women who will be killed tomorrow. They are going about their day, and I know if they were prepared to counter attack in the ways Loren Christensen and Lisa Place teach, they'd have a far better chance of prevailing tomorrow.

INTRODUCTION ■

Some "experts" say that you should be submissive when attacked at home or by a stranger. You won't find that advice here, although you might use it as a ruse before you claw his eyes and annihilate his groin. Your ultimate goal is to get away but you don't achieve that by being meek and docile. You get away by drawing on that hard-wired survival instinct that is ingrained into your every cell to attack him like an enraged lioness protecting its babies.

You will learn to use your hands, forearms, elbows, teeth, knees and feet to show the attacker that by targeting you, he just made the biggest mistake of his scummy life. You will learn that you're surrounded by a limitless cache of weapons. They are not a modern-day, high-tech arsenal but one that has served humans since the first cavewoman fought with a T-Rex bone to protect her children.

You're going to read the words "be alert, be aware" so many times in this text that they will burn into your brain—and that's a good thing. Because by staying alert and being aware of all 360 degrees around you, you're ready to deliver a rain storm of pain on anyone attacking you from any direction. Knowing you have the ability, the means and the warrior mindset to attack back will free that ferocious lioness that for millenniums men have tried to keep chained.

Understand that a stranger will attack a woman because she appears vulnerable by her bearing, and because of where she walks, jogs, socializes, eats, drinks and shops. He is convinced that she will not resist and that she will crumble under his assault. In short, he attacks her because he believes that he will be successful.

An abusive male partner usually begins by being controlling and possessive. Then he progresses to controlling the woman's daily activities. Where were you at noon? Why didn't you answer your cell? Who were you with? How long were you there? Soon he begins telling her what clothes to wear and discouraging her from seeing her family. The more he controls her the more she becomes dependant on him. Physical abuse comes next as does forced sex.

Although he might give a myriad excuses why he controls her and beats her, they are meaningless. The primary reason he does it is that he believes he can.

This book teaches you to show him that his belief is wrong. It will help you understand that you don't have to be submissive, tolerant and weak. You don't have to be a victim. You will learn that with a little knowledge applied correctly, you can be just as dangerous as the attacker is—even more.

Your authors have spent years training and teaching the martial arts, specifically, street survival. Their system is not about the study of a culture, spirituality, or a fun way to achieve physical fitness, although those attributes are a byproduct. Their primary goal is to teach people to survive a violent physical encounter. They know that when your adrenaline is boiling over, your heart is pounding like a jackhammer, and when you're gasping for precious air, the key to survival is simplicity. You won't find fancy moves in the first section of this book, "Physical Power." Instead, you will learn how to apply techniques based on natural movements, some as old as woman, some found in the animal kingdom.

The second part of the book, "Mind Power," is about how to use your head, not to headbutt, although that's a good technique, but rather how to learn, practice, be aware, be alert, analyze, assess, and use your fear as an ally. Mastering these things will help you avoid most violent encounters and survive those you can't.

An old white-haired master once said that one's greatest weapon is the mind. Absolutely.

An old Filipino martial arts master once took Loren aside and whispered words that are as simple as they are rich in meaning.

"If you practice very hard, you will be very good."

Let's get to it.

Note: We sent questionnaires to a dozen female martial arts instructors and asked for their input on a variety of questions related to women and self-defense. You will find their answers on separate pages before each chapter.

physical power

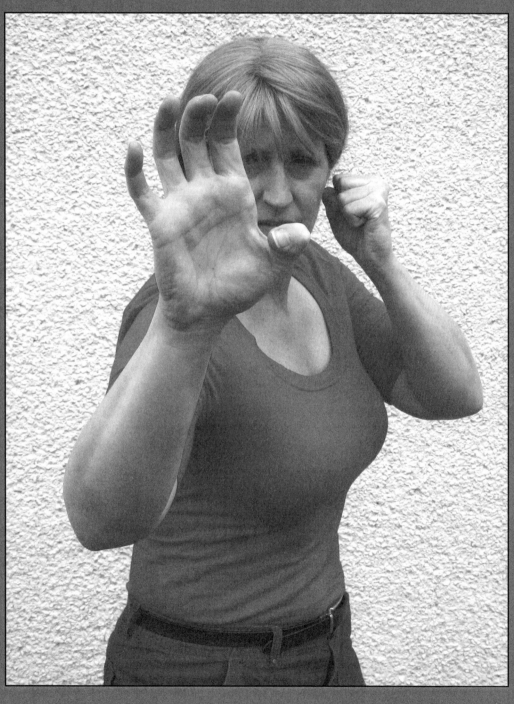

"To be effective in self-defense, You cannot just defend. You must *attack back*." ~ The Authors

Why should women learn self-defense?

The sad reality is that people would rather look the other way than come to your defense.

■ ■ ■

Emotionally, it's a horrible, miserable feeling to have been hurt by someone.

■ ■ ■

Because of our bleeding heart justice system, criminals are not deterred from doing crime. Essentially, the only deterrent is when the victim hurts them first.

■ ■ ■

A university study, I don't remember which [Brandeis University in Massachusetts, 1993], found that the women most likely to be raped or assaulted are those who don't fight back.

■ ■ ■

Just look at the statistics. You might not be able to stop the violence from happening to every woman out there, but you should take steps to stop it from happening to you.

■ ■ ■

At first, the force, power, and speed of martial arts intrigued me, and it was only afterwards that I had a real appreciation for it as self-defense.

■ ■ ■

I started out training thinking that it would make me less fearful. I soon learned that fear isn't going to go away, but you can learn to use it to make you a powerful force.

CHAPTER ONE

THE THREAT

The law calls a punch to the stomach, a slap to the face and a crushing bearhug an assault, whether the perpetrator is your partner or a stranger. However, for our purposes, we have separated the attackers into two categories, which we call "Threats by a stranger" and "Threats at home."

Threat From a Stranger

Loren once wrote an article about two homicide detectives who had just investigated their 100th murder. Both underscored that most of their female murder victims were killed because of their lifestyle choices: hitchhiking, being picked up in a bar, and walking alone on a dark, empty street. Sociologists say that stranger violence occurs in geospatial locations known for disorder: bars, taverns, rock concerts, drunken parties and other locations where unruly people gather. For sure, such places are ripe for arguments, conflicts, aggression and violent encounters.

Rapes, serial killings and kidnappings typically occur in isolated locations, such as jogging paths, parks, parking structures and empty streets.

Note: Why strangers attack strangers is a vast subject that is beyond the scope of this book. The interested reader can research other books on the subject or take college courses on sociology, criminology and psychology to learn how personality traits, drugs, alcohol, firearms, and cultural and regional values all contribute to violent acts. Our purpose here is to learn how to avoid it, deter it, and stop it with extreme prejudice.

All attacks, even surprise ones, initiate from one of the following five stages. Learn them, think about them, and discuss them with friends so that you recognize them when they occur.

Stages of an attack

Our friend Marc MacYoung, one of the most analytical writers on street self-defense today, has developed what he calls "The five stages of an attack," which he discusses at length in his excellent book *Safe in the City*. He has given us permission to talk about them briefly with a few modifications that apply to our subject. The stages are:

1. Intent
2. Interview
3. Positioning
4. Attack
5. Reaction

Color Codes of Alertness

The color codes are a simple but powerful strategy used by the police, military and reality-based martial arts systems to describe one's state of mind throughout the day. We reference it repeatedly throughout this book to remind you of the importance of being alert and aware at all times.

White Zone: You're relaxed, unaware, and unprepared. You're thinking about everything except where you are at the moment. If attacked, you will say, "He came out of nowhere." Or, "This can't be happening." When in the White Zone your only chance at defense is if your attacker is inept.

Yellow Zone: You're relaxed, but alert. There is no threat but because you read the newspaper and watch TV news, you know that something bad could happen today and you might have to fight back. People in the White Zone are unaware of the news or are in complete denial that anything bad could happen to them. When in the Yellow Zone, you use your eyes and ears to monitor your surroundings, all 360 degrees. You carry yourself in a way that others know that you're aware of everything. In time, this becomes habit.

Orange Zone: You've alerted on something. That person walking toward you doesn't look right. Something moved to your right when you got off the parking structure elevator. That man at the end of the grocery aisle keeps looking at you. The thought that you might have to defend yourself is in the forefront of your mind. You want to remain in this high state of alertness until the thing has gone away or you have departed the area.

Red Zone: It's on! You're thinking strategy. You're looking for an avenue of escape. You're retrieving something from your purse to use as a weapon. You know where your cell phone is. He is reaching toward you. You know what you're going to do. He is getting into your car. You know what you're going to do.

When in the Yellow Zone you can quickly make the transition to Red Zone. But if you're walking around in the White Zone, you *might* make the transition if you're lucky and the threat is inept. Most likely you will be unaware—until its happening.

If you're in an abusive relationship, you must be in the Yellow Zone at home.

INTENT

Because you're in the Yellow Zone, you see the stranger approach. You notice that he is looking from side to side and behind him as if he doesn't want witnesses to see what he is about to do. He moves even closer. Check out his body language: nervous facial ticks, hands opening and closing, feet shifting about, and a seemingly inability to stand still. These characteristics are not reason for you to attack him but they are enough for you to slip into the Orange Zone where your alertness and suspicion are on high alert.

You should:

- assume the leave-me-alone stance (see Chapter Two, "De-escalation").

- check your surroundings for weapons and an avenue of escape.

- extend your arms and say in a loud, commanding voice, "Stop! Don't come any closer." You might feel shy or awkward about doing this but do it anyway. It's all about giving yourself an advantage by being proactive in your defense, and about letting him know and anyone within earshot know that you don't want him to come near you.

- repeat your commands even louder should he continue to advance. Shout it if you think that is the best option.

- take the best avenue of escape.

- prepare to attack him with ferocity if you can't leave. Retrieve a weapon—pen, scissors, keys— from your pocket or purse. See Chapter Five, "Weapons, weapons everywhere."

While it might be uncomfortable for you to take the above actions, consider that not doing so could put you at great risk. A stranger, who is exhibiting common characteristics that we know are typical when an attack is eminent, wants to get close to you. He wants to "invade your space" so that he can do…you don't know what he will do. Don't wait to find out and be put into a position of playing catch up as you fight to defend yourself. Telling him to stop is within your rights and a wise move tactically. If he does stop, great. If he doesn't stop after you tell him to, that is one more element you can use to justify your physical response and one that can be used against him when he is arrested.

In his book *The Gift of Fear,* Gavin deBecker stresses that any person who doesn't hear your "No'" the first time ("Stop!" in this case) is trying to control you (and get close to you), and that when someone is persistent it means that they're troubled in some way.

INTERVIEW

When a potential attacker interviews you, he is deciding if you're a good target. This is one interview you want to fail.

Consider the just described twitchy man. As he approaches, he interviews you, watching how you respond to see if you would make a good victim. When you take a defensive posture and tell him, "Stop! Don't come any closer" and he does exactly that, you failed his interview. He sees that you're not a good target and he goes away, usually. But if you ignore his advance, as if it isn't happening, or freeze because you don't know what to do, you passed his interview; he now sees you as his next target.

Here are a few ways an attacker conducts an interview.

- He watches you from afar: your daily routine, where you park, where you go, how you carry yourself (timidly or confidently), and how alert and aware you are.

- He approaches and asks you for the time, directions, a cigarette, or to help with his stalled car. His true motive is to see how close he can get to you, how alert or oblivious you are, how you hold your purse, and to see if you're open for additional questions. If you're in the White Zone you won't notice but you will when you're in the Yellow.

- He approaches and asks the well worn, "How you doin'?" You answer him and he asks another question. "You from around here?" Or "Can I buy you a coffee?" Or he might comment that you look attractive, hot, or sexy. In short, he is interviewing you to see how you respond. He wants to see if you're shy, timid, afraid or flattered.

- He offers to carry your packages. He is checking to see how close he can get to you, to see if he can walk you to your car, or carry your things into your house or apartment.

Because nice people do some of these things, too, you must be in the Yellow Zone and use your well-earned instincts to know the difference. Be alert, be aware, and watch for any cues that make you uncomfortable. Is he talking too fast, looking around a lot, acting nervous, or excited? Is he pushy? Is he using his attractiveness? Is he charming? Uh oh, watch out for charming.

In *A Gift of Fear,* Gavin deBecker writes: *Charm is another overrated ability. Note that I call it an ability, not an inherent feature of someone's personality. Charm is almost always a directed instrument,… [it] has motive. To charm is to compel, to control by allure or attraction. Think of charm as a verb, not a trait. If you consciously tell yourself, "This person is trying to charm me," as opposed to "This person is charming," you'll be able to see around it.*

When someone asks you the time, you're under no obligation to stop and lift up your wrist or open your cell phone, and say, "It's 3:47." A better response is to keep walking, make eye contact with the guy and, without checking your wrist or phone, say, "About 4." Then as you walk on, stay alert as to where he is.

Likewise, when he asks to carry your packages for you, tell him, "Thanks, I'm good." If he tries to start a conversation, say something like, "Sorry, I got to make a call." Then, keep your eye on him as you call a friend.

The attacker who interviews you from afar is the type that people claim "came out of no where." In reality, only magician David Copperfield can do such a thing. The best defense against this person is to be in the Yellow Zone of awareness and alertness. Functioning in this mindset increases the chance that you will be aware of someone watching you everyday. But should he be watching from a position that doesn't allow you to see him, your awareness and alertness will detect him quickly when he does make his approach.

Here are some other types of interviews:

- The attacker seems friendly at first but becomes more aggressive in increments. He asks directions. After you give them to him, he asks you to walk part way with him. When you decline (as you should) he gets angry or insulting.

- He buys you a drink, which you accept (not a good idea), and begins touching you frequently as you talk with him. He might even comment that he is touchy person. In reality, he is testing you to see how you respond.

- He starts out aggressively: "You think you're too hot to talk to me, don't you?" He is testing to see if you will humble yourself to prove him wrong or if you will agree that you're indeed too hot to give him time. If you say no, he just learned that he can control you. If you agree that you're too hot for him, he might increase his aggression toward you.

Think ahead of time how to respond to these common interview techniques. Remember, you're never obligated to agree with him, give in to him, or speak to him.

"He came out of nowhere"

As a cop, Loren heard many stranger-to-stranger assault victims claim that the attacker came out of nowhere. He always wanted to respond with, "Really? This man, not a ghost, not a spirit, but a live person actually 'came out of no where?'" He didn't, of course, but the fact remains that people come out of *somewhere*. The attacker was there, but the victim didn't see him until it was too late.

To be fair, there are those occasions when an attacker does lie in hiding and then springs out to take the victim by surprise. Such was the case with Nurse Susan Kuhnhausen whose story we tell at the beginning of this book. Statistically, however, those incidents are rare. Most cases involve an attacker who is there and giving signals that he is a dangerous person.

Be aware. Be alert. Assess.

"He came out of nowhere"

POSITIONING

An attacker cannot attack you unless he is in the right position, such as standing close to you in a parking lot, leaning into you in a bar to—supposedly—hear you over the music, or helping you carry your packages into your apartment. He will use every ruse to get into the right position without making you suspicious. As always, your best defense is to be aware, be alert, and be in the Yellow Zone.

There are four positions in which an attacker(s) can do you harm.

- He surprises you: An example is when an attacker steps into your path from a darkened doorway. Hidden from view, there is no way for you to know that he was there. However, when you're in the Yellow Zone or Orange Zone you're better able to respond to the surprise. But when you're daydreaming in the White Zone…well, good luck.

Note: When walking at night, stay close to the curb and away from doorways. If there are parked cars at the curb, places where someone could crouch in waiting, walk in the center of the sidewalk. Better yet, get someone to walk with you.

- He closes in on you: In this case, you see the threat coming toward you in an attempt to get close enough to do whatever is on his mind. Because you're alert and aware, you see him right away, and you're able to read his facial expression and body language. Get away, step behind a car fender or a trashcan, and/or retrieve something from your person or the environment to use as a weapon.

- They surround you: You're surrounded when three or more threats encircle you so that you're unable to leave. The best defense is to be alert and aware enough that it doesn't happen in the first place. Let's say that you're waiting for the bus when you spot three undesirables moving toward you. React quickly by going into a store or any place in which there are people, by stepping out into the street to stop traffic, or by calling 9-1-1 on your cell and asking for a patrol unit.

- Cornering: Defense against someone cornering you in a bus stall, a hallway to the bar restroom, or against the railing in a high rise parking structure begins with—you guessed it—alertness and awareness: alertness of what the threat is trying to do and awareness of your environment. When you feel an impending threat, move to a place where they cannot corner you. In this case, move to the middle of the sidewalk, the middle of the hall, or the middle of the parking structure. If you're cornered anyway, you must explode like a bomb to get away: smash the closest attacker's nose with your hammerfist, shred his face with your claws, crack his shins with your kicks, and annihilate his groin with your shin. Do whatever it takes to get your freedom.

Position is paramount for the attacker; without it he can't hurt you, with it he can. Use your primary weapon—your brain—to stay one step ahead of him. Be aware, be alert.

Where Am I?

When Loren worked with rookie cops, he would occasionally pull to the curb half way between intersections and ask the young officer where they were. The first couple of times the officer would usually respond with, "Uh…"

Loren would ask, "What if something occurred right now, right here? What would you tell dispatch? How would you direct in back-up?" Loren knew what an awful, helpless feeling this was because he had made that mistake early in his career. It went something like this:

Loren: "Send more cops now!"

Dispatch: "To where?"

Loren: "Uh…"

It's great that you carry your cell phone but you also need to know where you are at all times. Do you know the names of all the streets on which you travel to work, school and the grocery? If not, learn them today. Then make it a habit to know the name of any new street on which you walk or drive. At first, this will take effort, but in just a few weeks, you will do it unconsciously.

Threats at Home

Two days after Loren got out of the police academy he stepped on a man's aorta. The hallway was lit poorly and Loren's attention was on the dead man crumpled on the floor, a hideous hole in the center of his chest.

Minutes earlier, Loren and his training coach had received a radio dispatch on a violent family fight, "family beef" in police parlance. A moment later, dispatch updated the call to "shots fired."

Chaos.

Shouting officers, TV blaring at full volume, a screaming woman, hysterical toddlers, cops struggling with a teenage boy, a choking cloud of shotgun smoke, and the coppery smell of fresh blood, lots of it.

Just before the officers received the dispatch, the stepfather, whose aorta Loren stepped on, had been beating the teenage boy's mother in the face with a heavy glass ashtray; it wasn't the first time. The boy tried to protect her but the enraged man knocked him down and commenced hitting his wife with the thick chunk of glass. In desperation, the boy retrieved a shotgun from a closet and fired it pointblank into the man's heart.

A week later, Loren and his coach got a radio call on a "loud family beef." The complainant was a neighbor. A large man answered the officers' knock and assured them that all was okay; he and his wife were just having a little spat. Loren's coach asked to see the woman to determine that she was indeed okay, but the man refused and started to close the door. In doing so, the big man moved out of the way enough that the officers could see the woman sitting in an easy chair a few feet away. Something didn't look right. When the officers tried to nudge the man aside so they could see her, he struck out at Loren's coach and the fight was on.

As the officers battled the man into the living room, down a hallway and into a bedroom, the middle-aged woman sat still in the plush easy chair, her arms resting on its doilied arms, her feet flat on the floor, a 10-inch kitchen knife protruding obscenely from her throat.

That was Loren's dramatic introduction to family beefs. There would be hundreds more over the years, most not as extreme, some worse.

This book is not about the complexity of domestic violence. (Check out "Resources" at the back of this book for a small list of reading material and websites on this important subject.) Our purpose is to teach you to be aware, alert, to diffuse violent situations, and to apply specific physical techniques to stop an assault so that you can get away.

Intuition

Much of human communication is nonverbal. It's estimated that as much as 93 percent of what we are really saying is done through our clothing, voice tone, facial expressions, hand gestures, posture, eye contact, and spatial distance. Work to perceive these things in other people, and pay attention to and heed what the information conveys to you.

Albert Einstein called our intuition "the highest form of knowing." Most of what we know about people comes from our interpretation of all that we see, not all that they tell us.

Be alert, be aware, and listen to your intuition.

The following are a list of indicators that you might be in danger. Knowing them and thinking about them will help you decide a plan of action.

Note: The word "partner" is used to refer to a husband, a romantic male or female live-in, or an intimate boyfriend or girlfriend who doesn't live with you.

You:
- Are you afraid of your partner much of the time?
- Do you refrain from talking about certain subjects because you're afraid of how your partner might respond?
- Does it seem that everything you do is wrong?
- Do you feel emotionally numb?
- Do you feel that you ought to be physically punished when you do something wrong?
- Do you feel you have to function in the Yellow Zone most of the time around your partner, always vigilant, always cautious?

Your partner:
- Does your partner constantly interrupt you?
- Does he mock your opinions and put you down, especially in front of others?
- Does he make you feel like you're dumb?
- Does he make you feel bad about yourself?
- Does he threaten you?
- Does he treat you like you're his waitress, personal assistant and sex object?
- Does he have a volatile temper?
- Does he damage your possessions?
- Does he threaten to take away your children?
- Does he threaten to harm your children?
- Does he force you to have sex?
- Is he excessively jealous?
- Does he have rigid gender roles?
- Does he call you or others to check up on you?
- Does he prevent you from seeing your family and friends?
- Does he control the money, phone, computer, car, and where you go?
- Does he abuse your pets?
- Does he like isolation and wants you to be isolated, too?
- Does he blame you for his problems?
- Does he have a negative view of women?
- Does he abuse drugs or alcohol?
- Does he have a Dr. Jekyll and Mr. Hyde personality?
- Does he restrain you from leaving a room, pin you against a wall?
- Does he stand nose-to-nose with you and shout in your face?

Note: Know that emotional abuse often leads to physical abuse. We define physical abuse as force that causes you physical pain, injury or in some way endangers you.

We encourage you to learn all you can on this issue. If you need help now, call the National Domestic Violence Hotline at 1-800-799-7233.

You don't have to live in fear.

WHEN TO FIGHT BACK AT HOME

Physically, a punch and a kick are just that, but the blows can carry a more significant impact when the person hurting or trying to hurt you is a partner. You might experience shock and disbelief that this person with whom you have shared so much and with whom you have made future plans would hurt you. You might feel betrayal because you suddenly realize that all that you had believed about your relationship was a lie.

On the surface, especially to people who have not been the victim of partner abuse, the decision as to when to fight back at home is an easy one. To those involved, however, emotions, the variables of each abuser, economic issues and the presence of children can make the decision extraordinarily difficult. For that reason, we reiterate that you call the National Domestic Violence Hotline number listed above and at the end of this book, explore the books and websites we've recommended, talk with your local police and with an attorney. All of these sources can give you solid information from their perspectives.

Our answer as to when to fight back at home is straightforward: You fight back the first time you're physically abused. Then you leave. This remains our answer no matter how complex the issues surrounding it. Problems, such as not having money or a place to go, pale when you weigh them against injury to you and your children.

Statistics

According to the U.S. Department of Justice, in one recent five-year period, there were almost 3.5 million violent crimes committed against family members, 49% of them against spouses, 84% of those spouses were females. Over three quarters of the victims of dating partner abuse were female.

Women are disproportionately victims of other violent crimes, too. According to the Stalking Resource Center, in one year 1,006,970 women reported being stalked. When the stalker was a current or former intimate partner, 81% of the women were physically assaulted by the partner.

The National Women's Study conducted a three-year longitudinal study of a national probability sample of 4,008 adult women (2,008 of whom represented a cross section of all adult women and 2,000 of whom were an over sample of younger women between the ages of 18 and 34). The study found 13% of adult women had been victims of completed rape during their lifetime, someone they had never seen before or did not know well, assaulted 22% of them. Husbands, ex-husbands, fathers, stepfathers, boyfriends, ex-boyfriends and other relatives raped 46%. Friends and neighbors accounted for 29% of the rapes.

Stats are important as they reveal the enormity of the issue but they don't show the horror, the fear, the humiliation and the pain.

THE UNPREDICTABILITY OF PHYSICAL FORCE

Our answer is based on nearly 70 years of combined experience training with physical force in the martial arts and, in Loren's case, nearly three decades working in law enforcement, which included responding to many, many domestic violence calls. One of the things Loren saw as a police officer is how the human body can be both amazingly resistant to physical violence and incredibly fragile. He saw people survive extraordinary damage, to include two cases in which the victims (one case was a man and the other a woman) were shot five times in the skull. Both survived; in fact, the woman was still running about and officers had to restrain her. Conversely, he saw people fall unconscious from seemingly minor blows, some even died. Rarely is there a way to predetermine how an individual will respond.

Many female victims of domestic violence told Loren that they were "only slapped," and begged him not to arrest their partners. Although we understand that there is much behind this way of thinking, which we encourage you to research, there remain dangerous ramifications to physical violence, even when it's "only a slap."

A slap or a push can be much more than the simple assault it suggests. Say you're leaning against a wall in your kitchen when your spouse draws back his hand to slap you. Know that such a blow carries with it a degree of force, sometimes great force when the deliverer is intoxicated, enraged or physically powerful. A slap to the face can knock you unconscious. A slap can easily knock your head against a counter edge or a refrigerator corner. Likewise, a simple shove can produce force that knocks you back a couple of steps or sends you stumbling over something so that you land awkwardly, break an arm, a vertebrae, or crack your skull against your fireplace.

You might say that that would never happen to you. Tell that to the tens of thousands of victims of domestic violence every year, many of whom have received life-changing and life-ending injuries.

That is why we say fight back.

BUT HE'S MY HUSBAND (BOYFRIEND, GIRLFRIEND)

Whether it's your husband, boyfriend or life partner, all the physical techniques discussed throughout this book apply. When you strip away all the emotion, history and potential future with this person, what is left is someone wanting to hurt you physically, emotionally and spiritually.

To reiterate, there are no special physical techniques when defending against a husband, boyfriend or partner. Since you know this person, you have an advantage that people dealing with the actions of a stranger do not. You probably know how he acts when he is angry, when he drinks, and when he tries to control and berate you. If he has assaulted you in the past, you might have an advantage in knowing how he acts just prior to committing violence. Think about these things ahead of time and include them in your preplanning and mental imagery practice (see Chapter Ten, "Mental Imagery").

Think about at what point you would use physical force against your physically abusive partner. This is something only you can decide. We can tell you that most of the women we surveyed said that they would use force against a stranger when he touched them. Since your partner touches you frequently, you must factor into your thinking how he does it. This isn't difficult as there is a big difference between a pat on the back as he walks behind you in the kitchen, and a hard arm grab, neck squeeze, or shoulder shove.

Although we can't tell you when to get physical, here are a few stages in a confrontation when you could. Think about them as to how they might relate to your situation.

YOU WOULD GET PHYSICAL

- when he touches you in anger.
- when he charges toward you, his face contorted with rage.
- when he has been drinking, and suddenly slams down his beer and charges at you.
- when he goes off like a cannon in your face and cocks back his fist.
- when he throws something and stomps through the house looking for you.
- when he tells you that he is going to beat you.

Do you have others?

As mentioned before, think about this before it happens because in the heat of the moment, it's hard to think clearly, make good decisions and know what is best for you. But when you think about it in advance and study the techniques throughout this book, you're more likely to react on autopilot before it's too late. See Chapter Ten, "Mental Imagery."

If you live with a volatile partner, your mind should be in the Yellow Zone of alertness whenever he is around you, or at least when he is in one of his moods. If he has an unpredictable and explosive personality, you must be alert and aware 24/7.

Better yet, get away from him.

Gavin deBecker writes in *A Gift of Fear*: "I believe that the first time a woman is hit, she is a victim and the second time, she is a volunteer."

Mandatory Arrests

Many states now mandate the police to make an arrest in a domestic violence situation in which one or both parties were hurt. It's a complicated issue, one that varies in nuance from state to state. Keyword "Domestic violence arrest policies by state" into your search engine to find out your state's policy.

Mandatory Arrests

Can women be effective at de-escalation?

Yes. I put a lot of emphasis on how to avoid the physical confrontation in the first place and on ways to defuse the situation.

■ ■ ■

Of course. Women are good talkers.

■ ■ ■

The more self-esteem a woman has as a result of her training, the more able she is to find the right words and actions to de-escalate a situation.

■ ■ ■

Learning right language and right body actions, such as gestures, distancing and facial expressions, will go a long way toward preventing a physical assault.

■ ■ ■

Yes. A good course teaches critical thinking about defense strategies, assertiveness, effective communication skills, and easy to remember physical techniques.

■ ■ ■

When someone tries to intimidate you verbally, understand that you might be fearful and afraid inside, but it is important that externally you appear focused, confident, relaxed and ready.

CHAPTER TWO

DE-ESCALATION

Loren used the following de-escalation techniques as a police officer and he taught them to others in the police academy. Do they work all of the time? No. When dealing with the human condition, there isn't any technique that is a 100 percent sure thing. That said, these simple techniques worked more times than not.

Leave-me-alone

STANCE

The beauty of this posture is that it has all the characteristics of a martial arts and boxing fighting stance. However, it's less threatening and it can even have a calming effect on some upset people. Here are the elements of the stance:

- Angle your body so that you're turned about 45-degrees from the threat. This makes you a smaller target and positions you to rotate your hips into a kick or hand strike.

- Your feet are shoulder width apart to provide you with optimum balance.

- Your knees are bent slightly, though imperceptible to the threat. This allows you to step quickly in any direction without giving away your intention.

- Hold your hands at chest level, palms forward. This is a non-threatening hand position that shows the threat and witnesses that you don't want trouble. When you make

Maintain a relaxed demeanor.

small, slow circles with your hands, some psychologists believe that it has a calming effect on some people.

- Maintain a relaxed demeanor. This presents an image of calmness, even when your insides are bubbling. A bully likes fear. Don't give it to him.

- Move slowly. This perpetuates calmness. A quick movement that isn't done for a good reason might startle the attacker and force him to act. Move quickly only when attacking, reaching for a weapon or fleeing.

- Don't point your finger at him or clench your fists before you're ready to smash his face. Pointing might antagonize him and fist clenching gives away your intentions.

- Don't touch a hostile person even if you're a touchy person.

- Unless you're deliberately reaching for a weapon, keep your hands in sight. You don't want him to think you're trying to get to a weapon when you aren't.

- To change your position, simply move the foot that corresponds with the direction you're going. For example, to move forward, move your lead foot a few inches and then move your rear foot up so that your feet are once again shoulder width apart. To move to your right, move your right foot first and then your left. (See Chapter Three, "The least you need to know" for a photo description of how to step.)

FACIAL EXPRESSION

Remove all expressions from your face. Affecting disgust, a hard stare, anger, or fear are like food to an attacker, food that makes him hungrier.

Remove all expressions from your face.

If the threat is your partner, call him by name without anger attached to it.

NAME CALLING

Don't call the threat a "loser," "idiot," "creep," or a curse word. To some, such words will inflame their anger (probably because they know they are true) and give them more motivation to hurt you.

If the threat is a stranger, you can't go wrong with "sir" or "ma'am." It might seem strange to call someone about to hurt you "sir" but it does have power.

If the threat is your partner, call him by name without anger attached to it.

Your Tone of Voice

How you speak is often more important than what you say. Consider these tips:

- Don't lower your voice too far below what is normal for you. Speak too low and he might think that you're angry or deliberately challenging him.

- Don't raise your voice too much higher than you normally speak because the threat might think that you're about to attack. The uncertainty in his mind might agitate him or cause him to attack when he otherwise might not.

- No matter how frightened you are, speak slowly as this can be soothing to a threatening person. It will help you to stay calm, too.

- In his mind, scaring and hurting you might be a way to get respect. Using "please," "thank you," "sir," and "miss" might be all he wants to hear.

- Using a humorous tone is always a risk. Since humor is an abstract, it's easily misunderstood, angering the attacker and escalating the situation. If you use it at all, and we don't recommend it, direct the humor at you, not at the attacker.

THREATS

Don't threaten. Don't say "I'm going to kick your ass," "I'm going to make you pay," "Touch me and you'll regret it," or "I'm going to call the cops." You might indeed do these things but don't tell the person in advance. It will anger him and he will likely take steps to prevent you from doing any of them.

GOOD WORDS

Using the right words can—meaning not always—diffuse a violent person. Dr. George Thompson wrote a wonderful book on the subject titled *Verbal Judo.* We highly recommend that you get a copy and read it three times. For now, consider these points.

- **Don't say** "Calm down." Never in the history of the world has this ever calmed someone. However, since it's judgmental and since it's usually shouted, it often provokes people even more.
- **Do say**, "It's going to be all right. Can you tell me what's wrong?" Or "How can I help?"

- **Don't say**, "What's your problem?" usually asked with a curl of the lip, ala Elvis, and in a tone that challenges. In a bar, it translates to: "Let's fight."
- **Do say** gently, "What's the matter? How can I help?" Or, "What can I do?"

- **Don't say**, "Watch where you're going you stupid jerk!" when someone bumps you.
- **Do say**, "I'm sorry. My fault." Say this even when it's clearly his fault. Hard to do? It can be. But say it anyway because by doing so the situation will likely pass and be forgotten. If you provoke him, however, especially when there is alcohol involved, the situation might escalate, turn violent and end up in injury, an arrest and a lawsuit. Swallow your pride. Life is too short.

- **Don't say**, "I'm not going to give you my purse you piece of dog ___"
- **Do say**, "Okay, no problem. Here," then toss it away from you and run.

- **Don't say** to your partner, "You're a loser. You always__." Refrain from starting any sentence with "you." And don't call him a loser, even when he is.
- **Do say**, "I'm sorry" even if you aren't. Say, "Please, let's sit down and discuss this." You're not figuratively pointing your finger at him but rather trying to take the wind out of his sails by admitting that you're at fault. You're also showing that you want to talk things out. Hard to do? Sure, you might be angry, too.

Here are a few more don'ts, whether the threat is your partner or a stranger.

Don't:
- challenge him.
- tell him that you're going to kick his butt.
- call him a name.
- curse at him.
- belittle him.
- tell him that you know how to defend yourself.
- say, "Come on, come on. Let's see what you got."
- ask him, "Is that all you got?" after he hits you.

The old "sticks and stones may break my bones but words will never hurt me" is a big fat lie. Words are powerful. Words can hurt, encourage, enrage, and instigate a situation, but they can also calm and diffuse it. Choose the latter. Yes, you might have to lie, swallow your pride and dignity, but by doing so you might buy time, distract and even terminate a threat's intentions. You might lose face, but in so doing you might save it—literally.

PRACTICE

Rehearse in front of your bathroom mirror or better yet, a full-length bedroom mirror. Assume the leave-me-alone stance and affect a neutral face. Check to see that your shoulders, neck and arms are relaxed. If your concern is an abusive partner, practice saying, "I'm sorry." "It's my fault." "Can we talk about it?" If you're thinking in terms of an obnoxious jerk in a bar, an aggressive co-worker, or a street assailant, practice phrases like "I'm sorry." "Can I help you with something?"

You will always have to modify your verbiage to fit the situation. This is especially true when it comes to your partner. You know him and you probably know what sets him off, and you probably know what calms him. We say probably because there are no absolutes when dealing with the human animal, even an intimate partner.

What techniques have you been taught that you feel are worthless for women?

Any technique is worthless if the woman is unwilling to use it. If a woman hesitates for a moment because she "doesn't want to hurt her attacker," which can happen under stress, she has given him the advantage.

■ ■ ■

Pulling away techniques generally do not work.

■ ■ ■

Trying to twist out of a tight grip.

■ ■ ■

No attacks are worthless, if you apply them with force and to the right target.

■ ■ ■

Techniques that knock the arms off generally do not work.

■ ■ ■

Women should be taught techniques that can be used in almost any situation.

■ ■ ■

Pressure point stuff on a big guy.

7 BASIC TECHNIQUES

The Least You Need to Know

A fox and a cat were out walking together when the fox began boasting how clever he was.

"I'm prepared for any situation," said the Fox. "I have a whole bag of tricks to choose from if my enemies try to capture me."

"I'm afraid I've only got one trick, but it has always worked for me," the cat said timidly.

The fox looked at the cat and shook his head. "One trick, how dumb is that? I've got hundreds of ways of escaping."

"I still think it's better to have one trick that works than waste time trying to choose from a dozen that might," said the cat softly.

"Rubbish" shouted the fox. "You're just not as smart as me."

Just then they heard a pack of dogs barking louder and louder as they grew near. The cat immediately ran up the nearest tree and hid on one of the highest branches.

"That's my trick," the cat called from high up in the tree. "You had better reach into that bag of tricks of yours and choose one right now or you're history,"

"Ok, ok, stay calm," said the fox to himself. "Should I run and hide behind the nearest hedge? Or should I jump down a burrow?"

The dogs were getting closer and closer.

"Down a burrow that's the way to go," said the fox, and started running around the field looking for a burrow. "No, that one's too small; I can't get down far enough. This one's too big; they could get down it, too. Maybe that one over there?"

Too late. While the fox wasted time, confused by so many choices, the dogs caught him and killed him.

The cat looked down sadly, and said, "It's better to have one safe way than a hundred you can't choose from."

The story of the cat, fox and dog is a fable about what can happen when there are too many techniques from which to choose. A British psychologist named William Edmund Hick conducted experiments in which people sat before a panel of random flashing lights and made choices as to which Morse code keys to poke. He eventually came up with a conclusion, which he humbly named Hick's Law. Hick peppered his findings with confusing looking formulas, such as $T = b \cdot \log^2 (n+1)$. Since we strive to simplify defense and offense, for our purposes, Hick's Law means this: It takes your mind longer to choose between multiple options than it does to go with just one. To say it another way, the fewer choices you have, the faster your response.

WHAT THE DOG, CAT, FOX AND HICKS MEANS TO YOU

Martial artists spend years studying the fighting arts, collecting along way hundreds of techniques, thousands when put into combinations. They don't need this many (imagine if all these moves were unleashed on one hapless mugger) but veteran martial artists study not just for self-defense but also for the beauty of the art, its culture, the science of movement, spirituality, unprecedented fitness, and its health benefits. For self-defense purposes, you don't need all that.

Self-defense is about simplicity. Forget anything you've seen in a movie that has the word "dragon" in its title and forget much of what you've seen in mixed martial arts competition on television. Yes, the latter is real fighting, but it's done in a ring with rules, a referee, a time clock, no-hit zones, and a complex set of techniques and strategies. While what you see in the movies and in competition is, in the broadest definition of the word, self-defense, the movies are pure fantasy and competition is too complicated and has too many restrictions (many of the techniques you're about to learn are illegal in competition). What you need are simple techniques and strategies that are instantly doable, easy to remember, and easy to do when your heart is thumping against your chin and you've got to go to the bathroom like never before.

A situation in which you have to defend yourself can ignite within a second. You're in your parking garage tossing your briefcase into your car when two powerful arms encircle you from behind, crushing the air from your lungs as you're lifted and then slammed against the corner of your open car door. Before you can cognitively process what is happening, your heart rate rockets from 65 beats per minute to 250, leaving your fine-motor skills in its wake. This means that a complicated defense isn't going to be there for you unless you have trained it extensively. What will work are gross motor movements, sometimes called "cavewoman techniques." We think of them as natural movements.

TECHNIQUES BASED ON NATURAL MOVEMENTS

The flashy tornado kick is an unnatural move. To do it, spin counter clockwise 180 degrees, lift your right knee as you come around and then leap high into the air as you whip your right leg in a high arc to slam your foot into the attacker's chops. Complicated? Yes. Needs tons of practice? Yes. Based on natural movements? Not even a little. So we're not going to do this technique.

Have you ever used the bottom of your fist to slam a tabletop or to beat on a door? It's a natural movement that no one taught you. You probably did it when you were a little kid. It's called a hammerfist and it's a good one for your repertoire because with just a couple of minor tweaks, it becomes one of the most powerful blows in the martial arts.

Have you ever kicked a box out of the way or kicked a lawn mower that wouldn't start? Some kicks are so natural that toddlers can do them not long after they start walking. Again, with some minor tweaks, certain natural kicks can be made devastating.

Training Cops

Loren has taught over a thousand police officers in person and thousands more through his books and DVDs. He doesn't teach them dozens and dozens of techniques because the students would forget them by the next day. Police officers are not martial artists, though there might be one who studies out of a hundred. Officers just want to learn a few proven moves to help them get through their shift so they can go home to their families. So Loren teaches a maximum of nine techniques.

Police Side-Handle Baton vs. Straight Baton

Sometime in the 1980s, police agencies began adopting a baton that went by many names, most commonly the "side-handled baton."

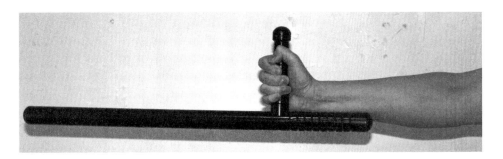

By gripping the short, protruding handle, the officer was able to deliver two or three times more whipping power and thrusting power than when using a straight baton. The brochures made it sound heaven sent, but many officers reported that it didn't do all that it promised.

There were two reasons officers had problems with it: First, they received only two hours of training. Second, the baton strikes and thrusts were based on unnatural movements. When a big drunken motorist decided to have himself a cop sandwich, swinging the baton by the little handle was so unnatural that officers were unable to strike with sufficient power to stop the threat. In the end, unnatural movements plus limited training time equaled poor performance. It took years of complaining, but the side-handled baton finally went away.

The straight baton is simplistic. Give a toddler a straight stick and she whacks her toy, her brother and the kitty, all without training. It's natural, it's uncomplicated and it's a gross motor movement. The police department now uses a telescopic baton, which is essentially a straight baton when it's extended. What is old is new again.

The good thing about the martial arts is that so many techniques are based on simplicity. The bad thing is that there are too many that are ridiculously complicated. Well, you will not find complicated ones here. Instead, we present seven simple techniques applicable to a variety of situations. We call them "the least you need to know."

Before we jump into the techniques, let's look briefly at how to step when moving forward, back, to the left and to the right.

Stepping

It's critical that you keep your balance in a physical confrontation since losing it can cause you to teeter or fall. Just as you must train your front kick and palm-heel strike, you must practice stepping so that it's there for you under stress. Fortunately, it's easy to do and won't take long to master.

Keep these three rules in mind.

- Never cross your feet. Crossing them leaves you vulnerable should the attacker move against you at that exact moment.

- No matter what direction you're going, move the closest leg first. This is generally faster and leaves you in balance.

- It's usually better to take small to medium steps than large ones. When your feet are far apart, you're in an awkward position to respond should the attacker move against you.

Here is how to step in the four directions.

STEPPING FORWARD

From your leave-me-alone stance (feet a little wider than shoulder width)...

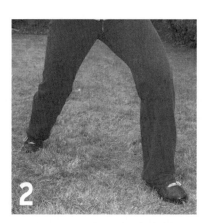

...move your front leg forward.

Bring your rear foot forward to assume your beginning foot position.

CIRCLING

When the attacker circles you, you want to turn with him, moving first whichever foot corresponds to the direction he is going.

- He moves to your right, you move your right foot first followed by your left.

- He moves to your left, you move your left foot followed by your right.

- He moves toward you, you step back, moving your rear foot first and then your front one.

- If you need to get a little closer to attack him, move your lead foot forward to close the gap.

STEPPING TO THE LEFT

From your leave-me-alone stance...

...move your front, left foot to the left.

Move your rear foot over to assume your beginning foot position.

STEPPING TO THE RIGHT

From your leave-me-alone stance...

...move your rear foot to the right.

Move your front foot over to assume your beginning foot position.

STEPPING TO THE REAR

From your leave-me-alone stance...

...move your rear foot back.

Move your front foot back to assume your beginning foot position.

Hammerfist

The veteran martial artist positions himself behind the large block of ice, and draws his arm up and back. Then with a piercing scream, he slams the bottom of his fist through the frozen mass, sheering the heavy block in half, and spraying frozen chucks and shards all about. That is the power of the hammerfist, sometimes called a bottom fist. It's arguably the most powerful hand blow in the fighting arts, though it's not often used in competition because it requires a large preparatory set-up that is easy for an experienced fighter to spot. However, when executed at the right moment to the right target in a self-defense situation, the results can be highly effective, even devastating.

When a movie character pretends to slug another with a knuckle punch, rarely do they show the puncher afterwards nursing a broken hand. The fragile bones that lie just beneath the surface of your fingers, knuckles, and the backs of your hands don't like it when you punch people in the jaw. Nothing good comes from hitting bone with bone. Meat and muscle, however, cushion the hammerfist. It loves to hit.

Right now, make a fist, lift it in the air about 12 inches and slam it down onto your thigh. That is a hammerfist, easy to do, easy to apply, and there is very little risk of damage to your hand.

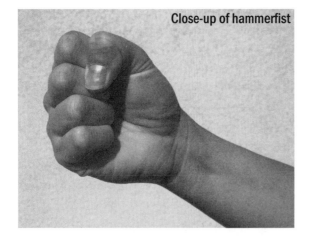

Close-up of hammerfist

THE CLOCK

Imagine that there is a large clock in front of you. Twelve o'clock is straight up from your face and 6 o'clock is straight down. Three o'clock is to your right and 9 o'clock is to your left. Those four numbers form a plus sign. There is also an X on the clock: 2 o'clock to 7 o'clock and 10 o'clock to 4 o'clock. You can hit with your hammerfist on all of these paths.

Let's begin with the vertical strike.

VERTICAL STRIKE

Assume the leave-me-alone stance, left foot forward, hands up, back straight. As always, your facial expression is neutral.

Turn your upper body to the right a little and raise your right fist toward 12 o'clock, as if you were about to throw a ball. Your left hand remains where it was.

Rotate your hips forward as you launch the hammerfist forward and...

...downward toward 6 o'clock. Stop at about shoulder height. Retract your other hand to near your jaw line or the side of your head.

Think Hips

When you don't rotate your hips, you generate only limited power. When you rotate them, you generate a lot more. It's been said that good hip rotation increases the power of a blow as much as 80 percent. We don't know how accurate that is but for sure you get more bang for your buck when you rotate them into the blow.

When learning the mechanics of the hammerfist, palm-heel strike, forearm strike and elbow strike, proceed through the motion slowly so that you learn to coordinate your hip rotation with the blow. Once you feel comfortable with the techniques, increase your arm speed as well as your hip rotation speed. Your hips should conclude their rotation at the same time your blow lands.

As your fist drops toward the target, rotate...

...your hips forward.

If the situation permits, rotate them a little farther to the left for added power and reach.

Expectations

In the movies, the heroine whacks the bad guy and down he goes. Real life is a tad different. You whack your attacker and he might slump to the sidewalk as he did in all your fantasies, or he might just stand there looking at you as if to say, "Don't."

Coauthor Loren Christensen is a 210-pound weightlifter who has trained in the martial arts since the 1960s. He has experienced both reactions. He once did a "sure-thing" technique on an attacker and the man just smiled, and said, "Didn't work did it?"

Never count on one strike to take care of the problem. While the targets discussed throughout this book are highly vulnerable, there is no accounting for what the human body can tolerate.

Therefore, never pause after you hit. If the target is still open, hit it again, and again. If the attacker reacts to your blow in such a way that the pathway to the target is no longer available, hit one that is. If at anytime during your attack you have an opportunity to flee, do so.

SELF-DEFENSE IN THE NEWS

Self-defense in the News: A man wearing a mask grabbed a Florida college student in an elevator. The young woman fought back, kneeing him in the groin and hitting him in the face. The man eventually staggered away, knocking over two motor scooters in the parking garage.

ATTACKER GRABS YOUR ARM:

A blow to the nose (pun intended) causes tremendous pain, watery eyes and momentary distraction.

An attacker grabs your left arm and starts to pull you toward his car.	Don't resist but step toward him as you chamber your right fist.	Bring your fist down as you rotate your hips to your left to deliver...	...a hard blow to the bridge of his nose. Repeat if needed.

DROP YOUR WEIGHT

Dropping your weight as you hit adds more power to your vertical blow. As is the case with rotating your hips, you need to practice a little to develop coordination. Once you develop the skill, and it will not take long, you will be capable of slamming tremendous force down onto the target.

As your fist drops toward the target (1), rotate your hips and (2) simultaneously drop your body by bending your knees. Practice dropping fast to add more power to your blow (3).

SEATED ATTACKER GRABS YOUR ARM:

You're passing by a seated man who grabs your arm to pull you down with him (1). Don't resist the pull but step toward it (2) as you chamber your fist (3). Rotate your hips as you drop your weight by bending your legs, and slam your hammerfist into the tender muscles of his upper forearm. Hit until he releases you (4).

The muscles of the forearm just below the crease of the elbow are quite tender and vulnerable to hard blows. With repeated strikes, his arm will be so numb that his hand cannot grip anything.

MULTIPLE VERTICALS

You're a human jackhammer, hitting fast and as many times as it takes to get the results you want.

Here is a bumper sticker for you: *If hitting him once in the face hurts, hitting him there multiple times must really hurt.* You can do it with the same fist or with both. When using both, be sure to incorporate your hip rotation to maximize your power. Know that you will not have as much rotation when hitting with your lead hand as you do when hitting with your rear.

From the 12 o'clock position, strike vertically down...

...toward 6. Notice the rotating hips.

Follow immediately with your lead hand, striking from 12 to 6. Note the hips rotate forward a little.

Hit again with your rear hand.

DIAGONAL STRIKE: 2 O'CLOCK TO 8 O'CLOCK

Use the same body mechanics as you did when hitting from 12 to 6.

From the leave-me-alone stance, chamber your fist a few inches farther away from your head.

Strike downward past the 2 on your invisible clock...

...toward 8.

As you practice, be cognizant of where your power is coming from and work to engage those muscles increasingly with each repetition. **Hint:** When standing, your hammerfist power comes from your hip rotation and from tensing your abdominal muscles when your descending fist is about a foot away from the target. On the ground, your power comes mostly from your arms, shoulders and core.

WALL PUSH

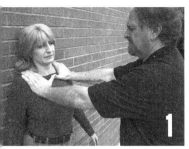

The attacker pushes you against a wall.

Chamber your fist...

...and slam it down at a 2 o'clock to 8 o'clock angle...

...into his brachial plexus. Repeat as needed.

Back view

The brachial plexus is a cluster of nerves half way between the side and front of the neck. A blow can cause confusion and temporary paralysis of the arm.

HORIZONTAL STRIKE: 3 O'CLOCK TO 9 O'CLOCK

From the leave-me-alone stance, chamber your fist as if to throw a ball.

Launch your blow from your right (3 o'clock)...

...to your left (toward 9 o'clock). Notice the hip rotation.

PULLED FROM CAR

An attacker grabs your arm to pull you from your car.

Yield to the pull as you chamber your fist. Whip it from to 3 o'clock toward...

CAUTION: Impact to the ear/temple area can cause confusion, dizziness, brief unconsciousness and, in extreme cases, death.

...9 o'clock, and hammer his ear. Hit it hard enough and his head will bounce against the side of the car. Notice Lisa's hip rotation.

Thus far, we have demonstrated with the right hand. You can do all the techniques with your left, too. You will be stronger if your right foot is forward when using your left hand because you can get more hip rotation into the blow.

The 2 to 8 and 3 to 9 "clock times" refer to when your left leg is forward and you're hitting with your right hand. When your right foot is forward and you're hitting with your left hand, the hours change to 10 to 4, and 9 to 3.

Whichever leg is to the rear, your corresponding hand is your rear hand. This is the ideal position for maximum power. It's not necessary for claws and eye poking techniques because power isn't a requirement for them to be effective. But to hit hard, you want to use those hula hips of yours and rotate them into the blow.

An interesting feature of the hammerfist is that when you hit in one direction, say 12 o'clock to 6 o'clock, you can also hit from 6 to 12.

Right leg forward, left vertical hammerfist

HITTING UPWARD

6 o'clock to 12 o'clock

Bend over and ready your fist to strike.

1

Hit on a path from 6 to 12.

2

ATTACKER TRIES TO FORCE YOU INTO A CAR

1

An attacker is trying to force you into a car.

2

Slam your hammerfist back,...

3

...up, and into his groin.

ON THE GROUND

Practice hammer strikes on your knees, on your back, on your side, and on your all fours. Don't limit yourself to any possibility. Here are two:

ON YOUR BACK

Slam your fist...

...into the target.

ATTACKER IS HOLDING YOU DOWN

The instant you have one arm free, slam your fist...

...into the attacker's brachial plexus in the side of his neck.

ON YOUR SIDE, GETTING UP

Ram your fist...

...into your imaginary attacker.

YOU'RE TRYING TO GET UP

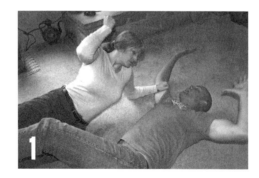

As you get up, you see an opportunity to slow him down from getting up, too. Slam your hammerfist...

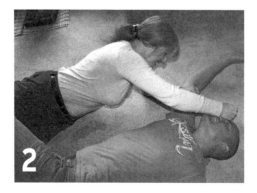

...down onto his nose.

Claws

Loren's recent books and DVDs rely heavily on clawing techniques, which target the eyes, mouth, nostrils, ears, Adam's apple, nipples and groin (see "Resources" at the back of the book). He teaches that clawing gives the attacker a different pain experience. For example, a palm-heel strike to the cheek produces skull-rattling pain that can discombobulate an attacker's thinking. Clawing, however, in which you rake your fingers across an attacker's cheeks, lips, nostril openings and eyes, produces a pain that burns, pierces and shocks the many nerves that lie just under the surface of the face. Likewise, if you punch or palm-heel strike an attacker's chest, he might or might not react. But when you use your fingernails to claw across one or both of his nipples, using a fraction of the power that you delivered with your palm-heel blow, he will grab at his chest and make a wide assortment of painful yelps. While pain is subjective from recipient to recipient, it's safe to say that most find the pain of a deep, ripping claw to have an intense, brain shocking effect. Plus, it makes it easy for the cops to find the guy once his face resembles a barcode.

Note: The attacker must be bare-chested or wearing a thin shirt for a nipple claw to be effective. If he is wearing a sweatshirt or heavy jacket, claw his face instead.

For our purposes, the word "claw" includes:

- Shredding: like a cat ripping its nails down a scratching post (or down your favorite slacks).

- Raking: a motion similar to a windshield wiper.

- Poking and gouging: what Moe was always doing to the other two Stooges.

You can execute clawing with minimum strength, space and body mechanics. Case in point: It's a fact that most mothers have been poked in the eyes while holding their babies. While these little people know nothing of proper body mechanics, all they need to cause pain and grief is a pathway to the target.

TWO CONFIGURATIONS

There are two ways to form your hand into a claw. Some people prefer just one and others use both.

FOUR FINGERS

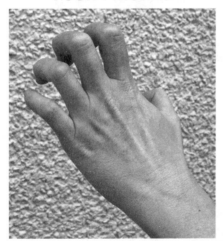

Position your thumb close to your palm and bend your four fingers slightly with about a quarter inch space between them. This tightens your hand and fingers, making them hard and strong.

FIVE FINGERS

Position your four bent fingers so there is a small space between them, with your thumb bent and placed relatively close to your palm.

SHREDDING

Imagine a cat on a scratch post. You can shred with one hand or both.

From the leave-me-alone stance...

...thrust either hand slightly above the attacker's eyes and then...

...shred downward.

YOU CAN ALSO SHRED...

Diagonally.

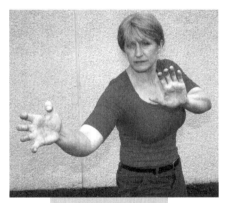

Horizontally.

Upward.

TWO HAND COMBINATION:

Right hand diagonal claw, followed by...

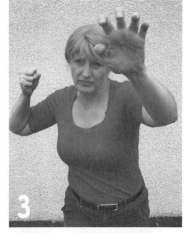

...a left hand downward vertical.

Clawing, shredding and poking the eyes can cause intense pain, heavy tearing and mental confusion. Deep penetration with the fingers might cause short term blinding, even permanent.

ONE ARM FREE BEARHUG

The attacker grabs you around the waist.

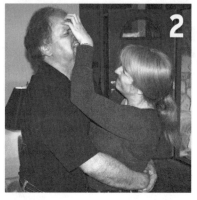

Immediately, use your free hand to claw his face from the top...

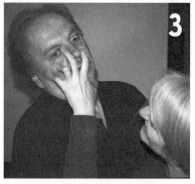

...downward through his eyes and...

...past his nose. Dig deep with your fingers and nails. Repeat as needed.

WINDSHIELD WIPER RAKING

We consider raking less penetrating than a shred. Target the eyes.

From your leave-me-alone stance (1) rake your fingers in a slight arc, right to left, across the eyes (2-4).

ATTACKER SPINS YOU AROUND

You can also windshield wiper rake him with both hands.

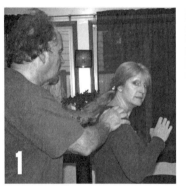 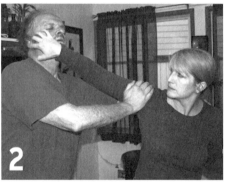 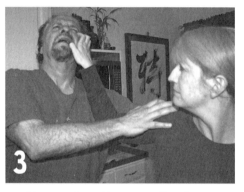

An attacker approaches from behind and begins to twist you around.

Greet him with a four-fingered rake across...

...his eyes. Sometimes your thumb snags a lip, such as in this case, and that's okay. Then in one, continuous fluid motion...

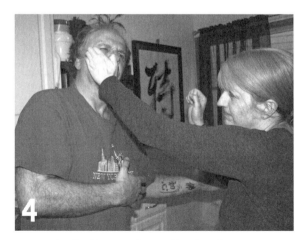 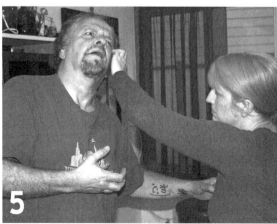

...rake the fingers of your other hand across...

...his eyes.

POKING AND GOUGING

Because poking and gouging penetrates more deeply than other types of clawing, there is a potential for eye damage, including permanent vision loss. Be justified to use this level of force.

From your leave-me-alone stance...

...thrust either hand out to make contact with the attacker's eyes.

ATTEMPTED BEARHUG

You tell him to keep away from you.

When he tries to grab you, push him back into something, a stove in this case (2). But he persists, ignoring your shouts to stay back. He growls that you're going to pay. "Now I'm going to kill you," he says. When he attempts to bearhug you again... (3)

...thrust your fingers into one or both eyes (4). Then flee (5).

ON THE GROUND

Practice clawing while on your knees, on your back, on your side, or on your all fours. Don't limit yourself to any possibility. Here are two:

ON TOP OF THE ATTACKER

Rip your claws...

...down his face.

ATTACKER IS PULLING YOU DOWN CLOSER

 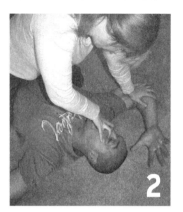

With your free hand, claw down...   ...his face.

ON YOUR BACK

Claw your fingers...   ...down his face.

ATTACKER IS ON TOP OF YOU

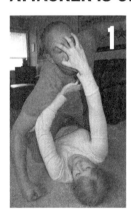 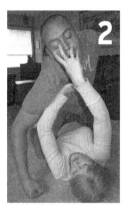

Claw your fingers...   ...down his face.

Clawing can be done from any position because it doesn't require the same power as does a palm-heel strike or kick. All you need is an opening to the target and an opportunity to get your fingers and fingernails into it.

Reluctance to Claw the Eyes

Some women have said that they wouldn't/couldn't claw someone's eyes no matter what the situation. For sure, there can be a powerful internal conflict about ramming one's fingers into the goo of another's eyes, even when that person is inflicting bodily harm on them. While the idea might be repugnant to you, know that an eye technique is most often a fight stopper.

The Army Special forces believe in the power of eye techniques. They train their troops to overcome their reluctance by having one person hold peeled oranges over their goggled eyes so that their training partner can get a "feel" for plunging their fingers into something that has a similar consistency. Loren demonstrates this exercise in his DVD *Vital Targets: A Street Savvy Guide to Targeting the Eyes, Ears, Nose and Throat.*

We have also taught students to thrust their fingers into the guts of a halved cantaloupe to get a sense of the sensation. Your training partner, wearing protective eye covering, holds the melon in front of his face, and screams and thrashes to add even more realism.

Fighting for real is an ugly thing and clawing an attacker's eyes is horrific. The time to think about it, the time to come to terms with it, and the time to practice it is now.

Palm-heel strike

The configuration of the palm-heel strike is quite simple.

Press your thumb alongside the side of your hand and bend your hand back as far as you can. Note how the position of your wrist and forearm support and stabilize the impact point, the heel, reducing the chance of a sprain.

While many instructors advocate hitting with the entire heel, we prefer to strike with the half that is on the little finger side, as it reduces pain and injury to the wrist when striking with great power. Turn your hand about 45 degrees in the direction of the thumb.

You can deliver force in three directions.

STRAIGHT FORWARD

From the leave-me-alone stance (1) thrust your palm-heel straight out and into the imaginary attacker's chest (2).

Your hips complete their rotation and your other hand pulls back to the side of your face at the same time your thrusting palm makes contact. This won't hurt an aggressor much but it will underscore your verbal "No!"

AN ATTACKER CONTINUALLY MOVES INTO YOUR SPACE

Tell the attacker to back away from you.

You step back but he ignores your request and moves toward you threateningly.

Slam your palm into his chest. Shout "No!" "Back off!" or "Leave me alone!" Flee.

DIAGONALLY UPWARD

A hard thrust to the jaw of a taller attacker jars the head and can affect confusion.

ATTACKER GRABS YOU

The attacker grabs your arm.

Drive your palm-heel on an upward angle...

...and into his jaw.

STRAIGHT UP

The attacker has pressed you against a wall so that you can't go back and you can't go forward. But you can drop down (1).

Lower yourself a little and then push forcefully up with your legs as you thrust your palm up and into his chin (2).

ATTACKER PRESSES YOU AGAINST A WALL

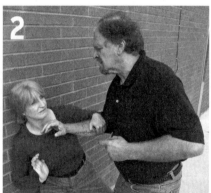

Close-up.

Because the attacker has pressed you against a solid object, you can't move forward or sideways (1). [The models are standing farther apart than normal so you can see the technique.] Drop down (2) and then launch upward like a rocket, slamming your palm-heel into his chin (3).

What, no knuckle punch to the jaw?

No, because of the risk of breaking your hand. Boxer Mike Tyson broke his hand in a street fight during his heavyweight reign and many veteran martial artists have shattered their knuckles after punching an adversary's jaw. Coauthor Loren Christensen broke his hand after a suspect deliberately slammed his jaw into Loren's fist (at least that is the way he wrote the report). Breaks to the hand bones, especially the little finger knuckle, are so common that doctor's refer to the injury as a "boxer's fracture."

The human skull weighs about as much as a bowling ball and is as hard, including the jawbone that forms the shape of a horseshoe. Why would anyone want to knuckle punch a bowling ball or a horseshoe? Use your palm-heel strike instead.

ON THE GROUND

Practice palm-heel strikes on your knees, on your back. On your side, and on your all fours. Don't limit yourself to any possibility. Here are two:

ON YOUR KNEES

Thrust your palm   ...straight forward.

YOU AND THE ATTACKER ARE GETTING UP AT THE SAME TIME

  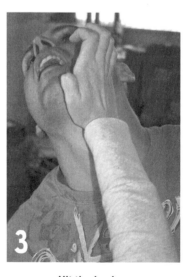

Drive your palm-heel...

...into the target.   Hit the jawbone.

A hard blow to the jawbone jars the skull and brain, causing pain, confusion, and possibly unconsciousness.

ON YOUR SIDE

Thrust your palm-heel strike...

...down into his face.

YOU'VE MANAGED TO GET OFF HIM

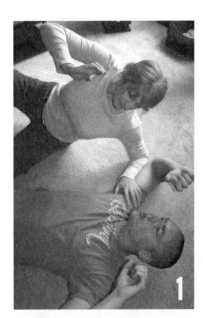

Ram your palm-heel strike...

...into his nose.

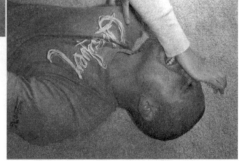

No, you can't drive his nose into his brain but you can give him pain, shock and heavy tearing.

Elbows

Look at your elbows. They are pointy, bone hard and scaly. Scaly won't help you much (try lotion) but the other two features will, especially when they are rammed into vulnerable, soft-body targets. Elbows are a close-quarter weapon executed in several directions: up, down, back and to the side. You can't rely on body momentum with elbow techniques so all your power is dependent on your rotating hips and torso strength.

UPWARD ELBOW

The upward elbow can be done with the lead or rear arm. The lead elbow is quicker because it's closer to the target but it lacks the power of the rear elbow that uses more hip rotation in its delivery.

REAR ELBOW:

Assume the leave-me-alone stance (1).

Fire your rear elbow forward and up (2) and strike the imaginary target to your front (3). Your hips have rotated fully and what was your lead hand is now covering the side of your head or your jaw line.

ANNOYING MAN PULLS YOU INTO HIM

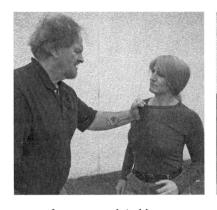 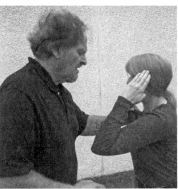 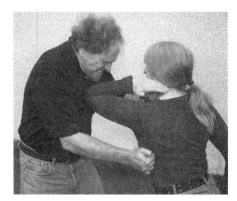

As you move into him...   ...ram your elbow up and...   ...into the attacker's chest plate.

Even among the obese, there is only a thin padding covering the chest plate, the area between and above the pectorals, and just below the neck. It contains many sensitive nerves that have a low tolerance to anything pressing into them, like that scaly elbow.

FRONT ARM ELBOW

From your leave-me-alone stance (1) ram your elbow straight up and into the target (2).

AN ATTACKER WILL NOT RELEASE YOU FROM HIS EMBRACE

You tell him to let you go, but he doesn't (1). Ram your lead elbow up and into his jaw (2).

Some schools teach that you should fist your hand when elbowing, while others say to leave it open. We have found that fisting the hand contracts the muscles, which slows the strike. An open hand contracts fewer muscles, thus allowing for faster delivery. Be careful, as it's easy to poke yourself in the eye with your fingers.

DOWNWARD ELBOW

The difference between the front arm and the rear is negligible, so use whichever one you like.

From the leave-me-alone stance...   ...lift your arm...   ...and drive it down into the imaginary target.

When the situation allows, drop your weight with the blow by bending your knees.

ATTACKER BEGINS TO LIFT YOU

During the course of a struggle, the attacker tries to lift you.

Quickly chamber your arm and ram it down into his face. In this situation, you can't drop your body weight so you must draw on your arm and shoulder power.

SIDE ELBOW

From the leave-me-alone stance...

...draw your arm across your upper body...

...and drive your elbow to the side.

Experiment to see if clenching your fist and pushing it with your other hand (see back elbow sequence) adds power. Some like it and others find it slows them down.

DO

Your elbow should travel close to your body to add stability to your arm and activate the muscles in your upper torso.

DON'T

When your elbow is far away from your body, it's unstable and incapable of delivering hard impact.

ATTACKER GRABS YOU FROM THE SIDE

The instant the man wraps his arm around your shoulder...

...chamber your arm and...

...ram your elbow into his solar plexus.

BACK ELBOW

From a neutral stance (1) extend your arm slightly (2). Then ram your elbow back into the imaginary target (3).

ATTACKER EMBRACES YOU FROM BEHIND

Just as his arms slip around you...

...ram your elbow...

...into his torso.

You can also execute this elbow variation by making a fist and pushing it with your other hand. However, as noted earlier, you might find that it makes you tense your muscles prematurely, which reduces your speed.

"GET BACK!" and other trigger words

Trigger words are short, powerful utterances that you shout as you hit the attacker. Choose words with which you're comfortable. "NO!" is always powerful as it's meaning is clear and can be shouted in a guttural fashion similar to an angry dog bark.

Your word(s) can give a command: "No!" "Back off!" Leave me alone!" "Kill!" "Get back!" "Stop!" or a curse word. It's also a powerful way to help you focus, forget your fear and bring out your inner warrior. Shout it each time you hit the attacker. "Back off!" Hit. "Back off!" Hit. "Back off!" Hit.

Wickus Booyse, a self-defense instructor in South Africa, has done a lot of in-class research on trigger words. He says, "The concept is sound. Since we scream under stress, we simply tap into it and use it as a technique."

ON THE GROUND

Practice elbow strikes while on your knees, your back, your side, and on your all fours. Don't limit yourself to any possibility. Here are two:

ON YOUR KNEES UPRIGHT

Drive your elbow up...   ...and into the target.

ATTACKER HAS KNOCKED YOU DOWN ONTO YOUR KNEES

Slam an upward elbow...   ...into his groin.

A strike to the groin can cause excruciating pain, nausea and incapacitation. That said, some men tolerate a hard hit to this target. As with all other targets, don't hit and then stop. Keep hitting until you can get away.

ON YOUR KNEES FACING DOWN

Fall forward onto your hand (1) and drive your elbow straight down (2).

ATTACKER TRIES TO PULL YOU DOWN

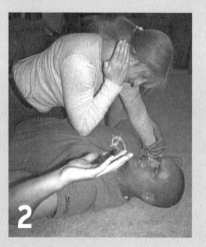

When the attacker pulls you down, extend your elbow...

...and spear into whatever target is available, in this case, the thinly covered chest plate.

Side Stomp Kick

The side stomp kick is a powerful weapon that you execute three ways:

• from a static position using just the power of your leg muscles.

• stepping forward to incorporate body momentum into the blow.

• stepping back as the attacker moves toward you.

You can kick barefoot, while wearing heels and when wearing sensible shoes. Since you kick at low targets—knees and shins—you can even kick while wearing snug pants and a skirt.

Your ol' butt-a-roo is one of the strongest muscles in your body, and together with your pile-driving thighs, forms a powerful partnership that can deliver major pain to an attacker's shin, knee or thigh. If you've ever stomped a cardboard box to flatten it you pretty much know how to do the motion. The only difference is that you kick to your side.

To examine the mechanics, let's look at kicking from a static position, one in which you don't move toward the attacker. You would also use this when standing fast and kicking a threat as he moves into your space.

On kicking

Many self-defense teachers advocate kicking techniques because the legs are the body's strongest muscles and allow for greater reach, meaning you can attack from farther away than you can with your hands. While these two characteristics are correct, there is one important aspect about kicking that you need to factor in. When kicking or kneeing, you're balanced on only one leg. Unless you're a veteran ballerina, yoga practitioner or martial artist, that isn't always easy to do, and never is it more difficult than when someone is attacking you.

It's paramount that you choose the right moment to execute your trained kick.

SELF-DEFENSE IN THE NEWS

After taking one of her children into a daycare, the 36-year-old mother scooted into her SUV and turned to look at her other child in the back. A man, whom she hadn't seen, took advantage of her open door to shove her from behind, and command, "Move over."

Before she could react, he shoved her again, repeating his demand. When she pushed him back, he punched her in the head with a closed fist. The woman was able to swing her feet around so she was facing the suspect and started kicking him and yelling. The man struck her several times in the head as he kept shouting for her to move over. The mother wouldn't give in to the attacker's demands and continued to fight and yell until he eventually gave up and fled the scene.

She said later that she had learned in a self-defense class to never allow an attacker to take you to a second location, as the chances of you being injured, sexually assaulted, or killed go up substantially.

STATIC POSITION

Stand in a normal stance, hands up and imagine the attacker stepping toward you (1). Lift your knee high to the front. You won't always lift it high when kicking, but it's a good starting point for now (2).

Use your butt and thigh muscles to thrust your kick out to the side about knee high (3).

Bring your foot back to a chambered position (4) and set it down (5).

ATTACKER GRABS YOUR ARM

The instant he grabs your arm and before he pulls you...

...chamber your leg...

...and slam your foot into his knee, thigh or shin.

Don't pose your leg in the air after. Set it down quickly to keep your balance.

MOVING INTO THE ATTACKER

Sometimes you might need to take a short step toward the attacker. The situation is such that while there is a small space between you and the threat, you're still unable to get away. Martial artists call this "crossing the gap" or "closing the gap." Stepping into the attacker adds momentum and body weight to the blow.

Your hands are clenched and you're ready to do battle.

Move your rear foot just behind your lead heel.

Chamber your kick by lifting your knee.

Thrust your foot out and into the target.

Retract to the chambered position.

Set your foot down.

IMPORTANT: Never step in front of your front foot as it's easy to trip yourself.

THE ATTACKER REACHES FOR A WEAPON

The instant he is distracted...

...step up so that your rear foot is nearly behind your front, slightly bent leg.

Chamber your leg...

...and slam your foot into his thigh (4). Return your foot to the ground quickly to maintain your balance (5).

MOVE BACK TO USE SUPPORT

It's difficult to kick while moving backwards because your momentum keeps moving your body as your stationary leg fights a losing battle to maintain balance and stability. Therefore, you must stop and then kick.

You might move back to:

- allow for an extra second to launch your kick.

- gain stability in your stance.

- use an object to lean on.

Assume your leave-me-alone stance and "see" the attacker to your right.

Step back with your rear leg and lean on the car trunk.

Chamber your leg and...

...thrust your foot into the target. Because you're supported, you're better able to kick higher, say to the solar plexus.

Or you can kick his knee or thigh.

A kick to the solar plexus can knock the wind out of the recipient and make it difficult for him to continue attacking. A blow to the sensitive nerves of the knee can debilitate his leg so that he has trouble standing on it.

ATTACKER GRABS AT YOU IN A PARKING LOT

Your initial reflex is to lean away , then you see a car fender behind you.

Lean on it for support...

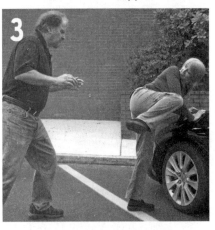

...quickly chamber your leg...

...and thrust your side stomp kick into his shin, knee, thigh or midsection.

ON THE GROUND

Practice side stomp kicks while on your knees, your side and on your all fours. Don't limit yourself to any possibility. Here are two:

ON YOUR SIDE

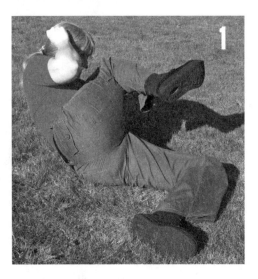

Slam your side stomp kick...

...into the imaginary target.

ON YOUR ALL FOURS

Thrust your side stomp kick (1) into the imaginary target (2).

YOU'RE TRYING TO SCOOT AWAY FROM THE ATTACKER BUT HE FOLLOWS

Chamber your leg...

...and let him have a little taste of your sole.

Hit with the bottom of your foot.

KNOCKED DOWN ON ALL FOURS

As he steps toward you, ram your...

...side stomp kick into his shin or knee.

Hit with the bottom of your foot. Repeat if possible. Get up and flee.

Front kick

Front kicking an attacker anywhere from his waist to his head with power, speed and balance requires lots of practice or a whole lot of luck. However, kicking lower targets, such as the groin, upper leg, knee, and shin is easy and natural; it's an action you might have used to get things out of your way in your cluttered basement or garage.

There are two impact points on your foot:

Kick with the ball of your foot (left top). Many women know this position as the "Barbie foot": foot pointed down with your toes pulled back to present the ball.

Kick with the toes (left bottom). Kick this way only when you're wearing heavy boots that are stiff and hard enough that you won't break your toes.

Here is how to front kick:

1 Assume your leave-me-alone stance, feet staggered, right foot forward.

2 Lift your rear knee while keeping your hands up.

Don't let your hands flail around as that will throw you off balance.

Do hold them in the open hand, leave-me-alone stance or clench your fists with your arms close to your sides.

Extend your leg and kick the attacker's ankle, shin or knee with the ball of your foot...

...or the toe of your heavy boot or shoe.

Retract your foot and set it down in back where it started...

...or set it down in front.

HANDSHAKE GONE BAD

You shake hands with a man but he continues to hold on.

You tell him to let you go but he ignores you. He gets one chance.

With your rear leg...

...slam the toe of your heavy shoe or boot into his shin or...

...the ball of your lightweight shoe into his shin. No matter the type of shoe, kick repeatedly until he moves or releases your hand.

The shin is one of the most vulnerable targets on the human body. It's thinly padded with highly-sensitive nerves just under the skin, even among obese people. A hard kick there will move the attacker's attention away from you and focus it on his pain.

ON THE GROUND

Practice the front kick while on your back, side, and on your all fours. Don't limit yourself to any possibility. Here are two:

ON YOUR BACK

Chamber your leg (1) and thrust your foot straight up (2).

ON YOUR REAR AND HANDS

As if you were pedaling a bicycle,...

...thrust each foot in rapid succession.

YOU'RE DOWN AND KICKING WITH BOTH FEET TO KEEP THE THREAT AWAY

Thrust each foot forward as if...

...pedaling a bicycle fast and hard. Get up and run as soon as you can.

YOU'RE DOWN ON YOUR BACK AND HE'S STANDING

The attacker moves forward with the intention of grabbing you. Slam the ball of your foot, or the toe of your shoe when you're wearing sturdy-toed shoes or boots (1), into his face (2). Kick with the ball of your foot (3).

Shin kick to groin

You can kick the attacker's groin with your front leg or rear one. Your front leg is faster because it's closer to the target while your rear leg is stronger but a tad slower since it travels a greater distance.

Don't kick with the front of your foot (the toes half) as there is no support there and it's easy to sprain your ankle.

Do kick with the top of the foot near the ankle or with your lower shin.

REAR-LEG SHIN KICK TO GROIN

Start in your leave-me-alone stance.

Keep your hands up as you snap your rear leg straight up and into the target. Hit with your lower shin. Return your foot back to the starting position or set it down in front.

SELF-DEFENSE IN THE NEWS

A 5-foot tall woman drew on all of her strength to fight a convicted rapist who had broken into her home and attacked her. "He came up from behind me and put his arm around my chest. I went to turn around, and he squeezed me real, real tight and pulled my pants down and pushed my head forward. I got the strength to get out of his hold and I pushed him. And when I pushed him, he swung and punched me in the jaw."

The attacker weighed 200 pounds but the woman didn't let that slow her down. She was determined not to be a victim. "I pushed him and he leaned over the front porch railing. And then I came outside and kicked him down the stairs where he landed on his knees. So I ran downstairs and I kept hitting him in his head and his face, and stomping on his legs so he couldn't get away."

The woman was also fighting to protect her three kids sleeping in the house. "I don't know where it came from. I was afraid he was going to get away, and that's what kept going through my head...'Don't let him get away.'"

A MAN GRABS AT YOU

Here is how to kick with the front leg when you need to cross the space between you. After you've pushed the grabber back...

...move your rear foot up next to your front one as quick as you can and...

...snap up your front leg. If you were closer to the target, you could kick with your lead leg without having to step up with your rear foot.

If he is close enough, you can hit with your shin half way between your ankle and your knee.

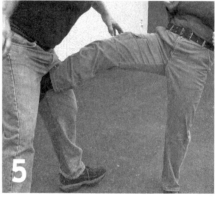

If he is farther away, hit with your lower shin near your foot. Be careful. Too close to your foot and you risk spraining your ankle.

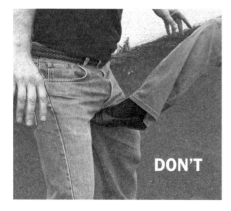

Don't: kick with your toes because it's easy to sprain your ankle.

ON THE GROUND

Practice the shin kick while on your knees and on your side. Don't limit yourself to any possibility. Here are two:

ON YOUR BACK

Slam your shin...

...straight up into the imaginary groin.

YOU'RE ON YOUR BACK AS THE ATTACKER ATTACKS FROM THE FRONT

When the distance is right, slam your shin up...

...and into his groin.

ON YOUR HANDS AND BUTT MOVING FORWARD

Scoot forward toward the imaginary target and...

...kick your shin into it.

THE STANDING ATTACKER IS NEAR YOUR FEET

He is standing a step away from your feet. The instant he is distracted...

...scoot forward and slam your shin between his legs.

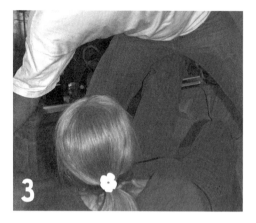

Kick through the target, as if kicking all the way up to his chest.

That's it. Just seven techniques: four hand/arm weapons and three kicks that will serve you well in all ranges and in most situations. Learning seven techniques instead of 15 or 20 is less intimidating and less confusing. In short, less is best.

In the martial arts, there is a type of student that we call "a technique collector." As the name implies, she wants continuously to learn new techniques, though she has yet to master any. In time, she is like the fox in the story told at the beginning of this chapter. She knows so many things to do, that she cannot decide which one to use when danger arises.

To be clear, we are not saying that you should not keep learning. You should. What is important is that you don't amass new techniques just for the fun of amassing new techniques. There should be a purpose for adding new moves, which we discus in the next chapter.

What other things should women know about physical techniques?

Some cardio kickboxing classes purport to be effective self-defense. This is neither true nor realistic.

■ ■ ■

Taking only one class will not teach you to defend yourself.

■ ■ ■

Learn from someone who has had real-life experiences.

■ ■ ■

All techniques must be simple.

■ ■ ■

For me, it's punching. No matter how much I practice, I will never have a punch technique that will truly serve me in a confrontation. I will far more likely do a palm-heel strike or elbow strike.

■ ■ ■

You should practice real-life situations with your partner.

■ ■ ■

A person can learn about techniques, but if their own morals or values would prevent them from using them, it is all for nothing. Each person needs to have a discussion in their own mind about what has to occur before they would use physical force and even deadly force.

4 TECHNIQUES

When you want to know more

If we were teaching a twice-a-week, on-going self-defense class for women, we would not introduce the material in this chapter until the students could demonstrate proficiency with the techniques in the last one. As mentioned, it's more beneficial for you to become highly proficient in the basics than it is to be a collector of techniques but lack true skill in any of them. Those presented in this chapter are excellent self-defense moves. Before adding them, however, we highly suggest that you evaluate your skill with the basic seven in the last chapter by using the following criteria.

Do you understand the body mechanics of each technique?

Are you proficient in the way you stand, rotate your hips, position your hands and feet, and use your eyes? Only when you can do all of these well will you get the most out of each technique.

Can you execute techniques with sufficient power to stop an attacker?

You don't have to be a Ms. Olympia bodybuilder to cause pain to the highly vulnerable targets we present in this book, but you still have to hit them hard. Too many women in self-defense classes don't hit with sufficient power to stop an attacker. You will when you follow the teachings in this book.

Can you execute the techniques hard and fast while keeping your balance?

Loss of balance often occurs when the all-out exertion of a kick or hand strike is mixed with adrenaline and fear. When there is insufficient training, such a blend can send you sprawling onto the floor. Conversely, when you train properly you will stay on your feet.

Can you execute combinations with speed, power and balance?

Train so that you can throw two or more techniques at optimum speed, power and balance. You're doing well when you can, say, throw a front kick followed by a left claw and a right-hand hammerfist strike without stumbling or swaying. Good balance means that you can throw another technique if you wanted, or scoot away.

Can you execute single techniques and combinations with skill in unrehearsed scenarios?

A prearranged attack and defense is one in which you know that the student attacker is going to try to, say, bearhug you, and you have to defend with a forearm slam to the face. In an unrehearsed exercise, all you know is that you're going to be attacked but you don't know how or when.

Do you know deep inside that you can hurt an attacker who is trying to hurt you or a loved one?

For many women (men, too, though they have a harder time admitting it), inflicting pain on another person is difficult for them to do, even when that person is hurting them. If this is you, it's pointless to continue to acquire techniques until you're convinced that you can deliver pain and suffering to another human being. More on this later.

As you can see, self-defense skill is about self-knowledge: understanding your physical capabilities as well as the inner workings of your mind. It's important that you're honest in your appraisal. Yes, you can do a nice palm-heel strike but are you convinced that it has what it takes to stop an attacker? Is it fast? Is it powerful? Can you deliver it with enough ferocity to do damage? Are you psychologically prepared to hurt someone? Can you feel the impact of your palm against an attacker's face and see his features scrunch in pain?

If you answer no to any of these questions, you need to spend more time on the basics and quality time thinking through any apprehensions you have about hurting another person before you collect additional moves.

Like those in the last chapter, the following are simple techniques based on natural movements. Let's begin with a classic.

Replacing Techniques

In our experience, the basic seven techniques suggested in the last chapter are easy to learn and highly effective. While these techniques are based on natural movements, it's okay to replace one should you find that it doesn't work for you.

For example, while the hammerfist is one of the first movements done by angry toddlers, you might have a bad elbow or shoulder joint that prevents you from doing the move effectively. Try swapping the hammerfist for a forearm or elbow strike. Or perhaps you can't do the very natural side stomp kick because of a hip problem. Try replacing it with the knee strike since it involves a different hip action and muscle group. If that hurts your hips, consider adding another hand technique from this chapter.

The goal is to build a simple, natural and easy-to-do cache of body weapons.

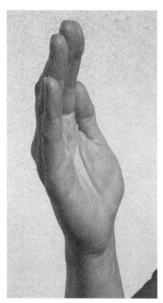

The Slap

If there was ever an underrated self-defense technique it's the slap, not just any slap, but a well trained one. It's surprisingly powerful because of the tremendous force generated by your hips. You can do it with either hand, though there is more power in your rear hand and more speed in your lead. We discuss these features further as we proceed. First, the mechanics:

Cup your hand slightly, bend your fingers a little, and press your thumb against the side of your hand. This hardens your weapon, while keeping your thumb from catching on something and breaking. Cupping your hand creates a vacuum, which is especially effective when striking an ear.

REAR HAND

Assume the leave-me-alone stance.	Launch your rear open hand...	...in a circular motion into the target (notice the turning hips)...	...to your front.

There are two drawbacks to slapping:

Because it's an easy-to-see movement, you must choose the right moment so the attacker can't block or grab your arm.

The impact might hurt (sting) your hand.

DEFENSE AGAINST AN ATTACKER PULLING YOU

An attacker grabs your arm and pulls you toward his car.

Your intent is to slap his ear but he suddenly looks off to the side. Better yet.

Use his pull to add momentum to your blow. Whip your slap...

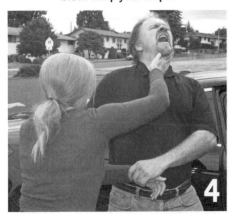

...into his Adam's apple. Break loose and flee.

LEAD HAND

Because there is less assistance from your hips when doing a lead-hand strike and the distance to the target is shorter (less time to build force) than when striking with the rear hand, many people don't have enough body strength to deliver sufficient impact. If this is you, but it's the only technique available at the moment, slap anyway to at least distract the attacker or to set him up for another stronger technique.

From your leave-me-alone stance...

...whip your lead palm...

...into the target.

ON THE GROUND

ON YOUR SIDE, LEANING ON ONE FOREARM

Slap your palm (1) down onto the target (2).

STRADDLING THE ATTACKER

Whip your slap...   ...into the target.

YOU HAVE JUST BROKEN AWAY

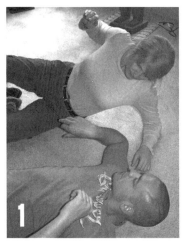

Before he can get up, whip your palm down (1) onto his throat (2).

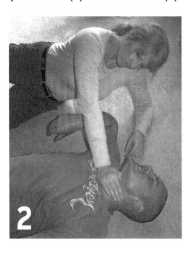

YOU'RE FIGHTING THE ATTACKER

Whip your palm down (1) and into his ear (2).

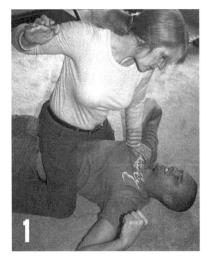

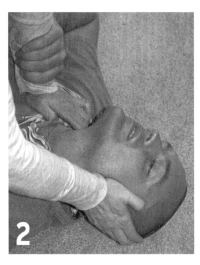

Forearm Strike

If you've never considered your forearm to be a weapon, you're in for a pleasant surprise. Pleasant for you but not so pleasant for El Creepo.

Advantages of the forearm strike

- There is minor preparation: no chambering, no cocking, no wind-up. Mostly, you just decide to do it, and do it.

- When thrusting, you can augment with your other hand to add more muscle and bodyweight into the blow.

- When delivered to a soft target—neck, nose, groin—there is little risk of injury to your arm.

- The stronger your arms and chest, the more impact you can deliver.

Disadvantages of the forearm strike

- If this technique is new to you, you must practice extra hard to ingrain its usefulness into your mind.

- You must remember to hit soft targets to prevent injury to your arm.

OUTSIDE FOREARM: AUGMENTED THRUST

Assume the leave-me-alone stance.

Fist your lead hand and move your arm across your body.

Press your other hand against your lower forearm as you thrust forward.

A MAN AT A PARTY PREVENTS YOU FROM PASSING

You've asked him twice to let you pass but he refuses (1). Lunge forward with your lead foot and thrust your augmented forearm (2)...

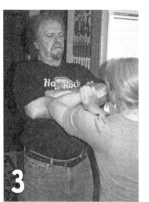

...into his arms (3). If needed, step up with your rear foot (4)...

...and then step forward again with your lead (5) to drive him through the doorway (6).

The augmented thrust and push relies on the muscles of your upper body, core, arms and your thighs. See Chapter Seven, "Getting strong now." Strong is best.

OUTSIDE FOREARM: SLAM

This is similar to the augmented thrust except it's not, well, augmented. It's a little faster but since it's a single arm action, it's not as powerful. Think of this version as a fast snap and the augmented one as a powerful thrust.

Assume your leave-me-alone stance.

Quick as a blink, snap your lead forearm up...

...and into the target.

ATTACKER TRIES TO GRAB YOU

The attacker reaches to pull or push you.

Slap his hand aside.

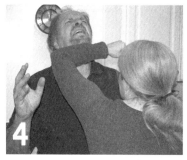

From where your slap ends, thrust your forearm into his face or throat.

If there is a path to these targets without having to knock his hands aside, simply ram your outer forearm into the target.

INSIDE FOREARM: WHIP

Some people might think that the inside forearm whip is a tad strange. For sure, it's rarely seen in women's self-defense classes and most other martial arts training, as well. That doesn't mean it's ineffective; it means it's not well known. Loren has used it for years and has taught it in other books. It's ideal for those moments when you're so close to the attacker that other techniques are impossible to do. It requires only two things: a free arm and an exposed target. As always, strong arms make the blow even more debilitating.

   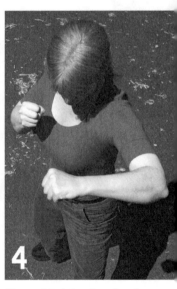

Assume the leave-me-alone stance.	Shoot either arm out, let's make it the lead,...	...until it reaches full extension.	Then whip it back as hard as you can into the target.

AN ATTACKER PULLS YOU INTO HIM

 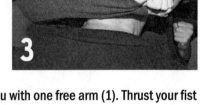

A man pulls you into him, leaving you with one free arm (1). Thrust your fist out (2) and whip your inner forearm into the back of his neck or the boney ridge just above it (3). Repeat until he frees you.

A hard blow to the back of the neck causes pain, confusion and dizziness. A blow to the external occipital protuberance, that boney ridge on the back of the head, also causes great pain, dizziness and mental confusion.

ON THE GROUND

Practice forearm strikes while on the ground, on your knees and on your all fours. Don't limit yourself to any possibility. Here are two:

ON ALL FOURS

Ram your forearm (1) straight down into the front of the throat (2).

> A blow to the front of the throat can cause extreme pain, choking and death. Be justified to use this level of force.

YOU'VE MANAGED TO GET ON TOP OF THE ATTACKER

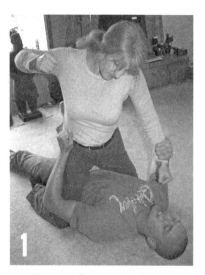

Use your free arm to slam...

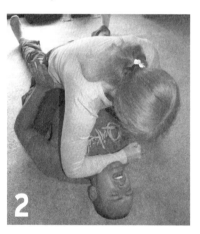

...it down into his throat or face.

ON YOUR BACK

Ram your supported forearm...

...up and into the target.

THE ATTACKER IS ON TOP OF YOU

Shoot your supported forearm up and...

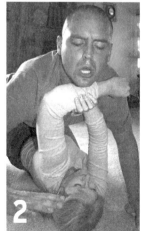

...into his throat. If only one arm is free, hit him with an unsupported forearm.

Stomp

Have you ever stomped your foot in anger? It's a natural move, one that can be made more powerful for self-defense purposes with just a minor tweak.

DRIVE YOUR ENERGY DOWNWARD

Have you ever watched five-year-olds stomp on bugs? They drop their entire weight down onto the hapless little critters. As they get older, however, they stand upright to carry out their cruelty. Sometimes they stomp downward with their lower bodies while lifting their upper bodies. This doesn't make a difference to an ant, but when done on a human attacker, the opposing actions divide the force. It's an easy habit to develop; fortunately, it's an easy one to fix.

The last thing the attacker sees.

DON'T:

Stomp your foot...

...down and simultaneously lift your upper body. This common error divides your force.

DO:

Lift your foot...

...and slam your foot down. Drop your body down with the stomp to drive as much of your weight into the blow as possible.

THE ATTACKER TAKES YOU DOWN

The attacker has taken you to the ground. You manage to break away and you're getting up.

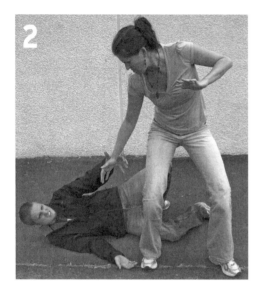

He starts to get up, too (2). Chamber your leg (3)...

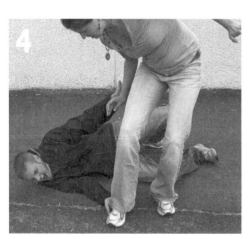

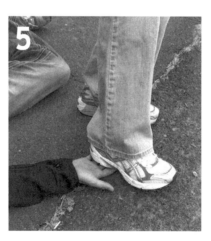

...and stomp your heel down onto his fingers (4). Stomping the palm hurts, but stomping the fingers hurts more (5).

ON THE GROUND

Practice the stomp while on your knees, your back, your side, and on all fours. Don't limit yourself to any possibility. Here are two:

SITTING

Get up from sitting on your hip...

...and stomp...

...down onto the target.

YOU'RE TRYING TO GET UP

You see his knee right there in front of you.

To prevent him from getting up, lift your knee high...

...and slam your foot onto his kneecap.

YOU'RE ON YOUR ALL FOURS

From your hands and knees...

...chamber your knee...

...and stomp it downward.

YOU'VE ROLLED OFF THE ATTACKER AND YOU NEED TO PREVENT HIM FROM GRABBING YOU

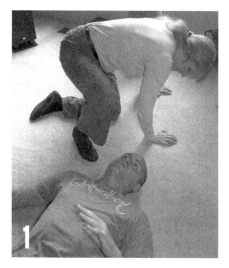

From your hands and knees...

...chamber your knee...

...and slam your foot down onto his face.

Knee strike

A knee strike is similar to a bullet: it hurts no matter where it hits. Okay, it's not quite like a bullet but it nonetheless hurts something awful even when the recipient tries to block it. Here is why:

- Your leg muscles are extremely powerful (even more so when you practice the squats in Chapter Seven, "Getting strong now") and thus capable of delivering tremendous impact.

- Your patella, or kneecap, is a large bone designed by nature to protect the inner workings of your knee joint…as well as to crush an attacker's groin or nose.

Let's begin by looking at two ways to deliver a knee strike: 1) on a straight path forward; 2) on a circular path forward. You can use your front leg or rear one. As is the case with front and rear hand techniques, the front knee is a little faster because it's closer to the target. Your rear leg is more powerful because it incorporates hip rotation and travels a greater distance, allowing it to gather impact force along the way.

FRONT-LEG STRAIGHT KNEE

Although your front knee has less power than your rear one, when you're close to the attacker you can still deliver enough pain to stop or momentarily distract him.

Your feet are slightly staggered and your arms are down at your sides or in front of your chest as if being restrained.

Thrust off your front foot and drive your knee straight up.

If his grip is loose enough, thrust your hips forward to get even more penetration.

THE ATTACKER IS RESTRAINING YOU, YOUR ARMS PINNED BETWEEN YOU

He is holding you against him.

Bring your knee straight up and into the groin as if trying to drive it all the way to his chin.

Leaning back a little (not too much) helps to ram your knee in even harder.

REAR STRAIGHT KNEE

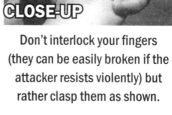

Don't interlock your fingers (they can be easily broken if the attacker resists violently) but rather clasp them as shown.

Stand in your leave-me-alone stance (1) . You can deliver a rear-leg knee strike by taking a lead-leg step as pictured, or without taking one (2). Extend your arms and clasp your hands together palm-to-palm behind the attacker's neck (3). Drive your elbows into his collarbones (this isn't always possible) for leverage as you pull down on his neck with your hands (4). Drive your rear knee up (5) and into the target. Notice how the knee penetrates (6). Depending on the position of your bodies, your elbow might not make contact with him.

A MAN PULLS YOU INTO HIM

He grabs your shoulders. Instead of resisting his strong pull, yield to it (1).

The bladder, located just above the groin, is a wealth of sensitive nerves. When struck, the recipient feels a collection of painful sensations, leaving him wondering if he is going to vomit, urinate or defecate.

Clasp your hands behind his neck and brace your elbows against him (2). If for whatever reason you're unable to get to his neck, grab his shoulders or a wad of his clothes. You cannot place your elbows against him when grabbing lower than the neck (3).

Three things happen simultaneously (4): 1) You pull the attacker toward you; 2) you thrust your hips forward; 3) and you ram your knee into his bladder. Pulling his neck or grabbing his shoulders or clothing provides you with good leverage, and allows you to pull him into your blow. If you cannot grab anything, knee him to distract, and then grab something and knee him a few more times.

ROUND KNEE STRIKE

The round knee strike travels in an arc. While it's commonly used to hit the side of the torso, we show you how to use it against other targets, too.

LEAD-LEG ROUND KNEE

As with the straight knee strike, the lead-leg round is less powerful than the rear but it's quicker because of its closer proximity to the target.

You don't always get the chance to step up with your rear foot, but do it when you can to increase your power. Be sure to turn your rear foot out a little, which allows your round knee to travel in a larger arc.

Clasping your hands behind his neck is ideal but if you can't, grab his shirt collar as shown. Sometimes you can't grab anything (1). Lift your front knee hard and fast (2), and ram it through the target (3).

A MAN HAS GRABBED THE FRONT OF YOUR SHIRT

The instant he grabs you...

... step up with your rear foot (you're unable to grab anything on his upper body)...

...and ram your lead knee...

...into the most available target. In this case, it's the highly sensitive peroneal nerve located at the side of the leg.

The peroneal nerve extends from the hip down to the knee on the outside of the leg. If he were wearing uniform pants with a stripe on the side of the pantleg, it would be directly underneath. A hard blow about one third of the way down from the hip as pictured can cause extreme pain and debilitation of the leg.

HOW TO DO REAR-LEG ROUND KNEE

From the leave-me-alone stance (1) step forward and reach for the attacker's neck. Or just reach forward if you can't take a step. Clasp your palms together and brace your elbows against his chest. Pivot your lead foot out a little so that you can rotate your hips (2). Drive off your rear foot to launch your knee (3) around and into the target (4).

YOU'RE STRUGGLING WITH AN ATTACKER

You're fighting for dominance (1) when for one brief moment most of your weight is on your lead foot. Grab what you can on his upper body (2). Pivot your front foot a little, as you drive off your rear one (3). Ram your knee into the front of his body, his bladder in this case. You could also hit higher to his solar plexus or lower to his groin (4).

VARIATION

When standing in front of the attacker, drive your knee into his side.

During the struggle, you latch onto an attacker standing directly in front of you (1). Drive off your rear foot and slam your knee into his lower ribs (2).

A blow to the lower ribs, just above the hipbone, is painful and can knock the wind out of the recipient.

ON THE GROUND

Practice knee strikes while on your side or when dropping downward. Don't limit yourself to any possibility. Here are two:

WHEN FORCED DOWN

From a standing position, drop your knee (1) down into the target (2).

ATTACKER GRABS YOUR ANKLE

You have gotten up first but the attacker grabs your ankle (1). Drop your knee along with your full body weight into the side of his head. Because his head is braced on the floor, it absorbs the full energy of the drop (2).

ON YOUR SIDE

Simulate grabbing the attacker and drive your knee...

...into the best available target.

SIDE STRUGGLE

During the course of a struggle, seize an opening to grab the attacker's head (1) . Ram your knee into his supported skull (2) repeatedly until you can get away (3).

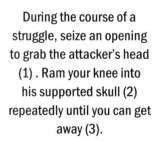
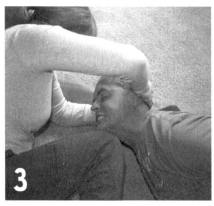

How important are common everyday objects for self-defense?

A woman's purse is an arsenal of weapons. I like to take a woman's purse in class and show everyone all the potential weapons she is carrying around.

■ ■ ■

When my husband and I first moved into our house, three men forced their way into our backyard, yelling obscenities and threats, believing that the previous owner still lived in the house. Although we have hundreds of martial arts weapons, none of them had been unpacked yet. I grabbed a hammer and waited, somewhat in a daze, as if I was not sure if it all was a dream.

■ ■ ■

I teach that anything can be a weapon. I read once about a woman defending herself with a zucchini.

■ ■ ■

I teach women to look around in each room in her house at all the possible weapons that are available.

■ ■ ■

Carry an alcohol-based spray in your purse, like hairspray, perfume, and hand sanitizer.

CHAPTER FIVE

WEAPONS

Weapons Everywhere

You've seen movies where the female is alone in her house when she hears a noise outside the front door. Her eyes widen and she clutches her hands to her chest. As the camera moves in to capture her stark terror, ominous silhouettes move across a curtained window behind. She turns toward them, her face contorted in fear as she nearly rubs the skin off her hands. She dashes into the kitchen, stopping short when the backdoor doorknob turns first one way, and then the other. Oh how helpless she is! How vulnerable!

Hardly.

When we watch such a movie, we shout at the screen (at home, not in a theater) "Hello? Pick up the fireplace poker!" "Grab the table lamp!" "Hey, the kitchen is full of knives, iron skillets and a food blender!" "Turn on the oven to 'Bake" and push him inside!" Well, maybe not the last one. But then again, if he's short…

SELF-DEFENSE IN THE NEWS

A 24-year-old man used a hammer to smash through the back door of a house where a woman lived with her two young children. She quickly armed herself with a knife and moved so that a table was between her and the violent intruder. He subsequently stole her van keys and led police on a high-speed chase. When forced to stop, he fled on foot and when cornered, resisted arrest with a box cutter. He injured two officers before being taken into custody.

It's not hard to turn common household items into dynamic weapons of self-defense. Consider the fireplace poker. In the movie *Zorro*, Don Diego, played by Anthony Hopkins asked Alejandro Murrieta, played by Antonio Banderas if he knew how to use a sword. Alejandro answered, "Yes, the pointy end goes into the other man." Likewise with the other household items: The lamp goes into the man's face. The kitchen knife goes into the man's shoulder. The iron skillet goes upside the man's ear.

Right now, improvised weapons surround you, and we can say this without knowing where you're reading this. At first, you might have to think about it a little when considering an object, but after a couple of days, you will do it quickly, no matter where you are.

Before we consider all the potential weapons around you, let's categorize them.

TYPES OF IMPROVISED WEAPONS

Here are the types and examples of each. Look around you right now.

Edged weapons

- o knife, metal-edged ruler, corner of a CD box, cheese grater, scissors
- o Ram a DVD box into the attacker's face (1).
- o Swipe a cheese grater across his face (2).

 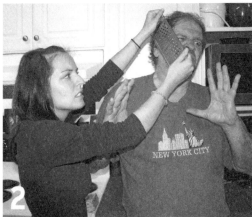

Pointed weapons

- o knife, pin, pen, pencil, fork, staple, pointy ceramic
- o Stab your pen into his arm (3).
- o Hit him with the pointy end of a figurine (4).

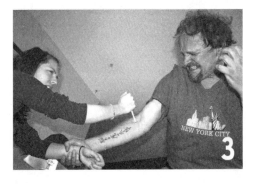 

Impact weapons

- o purse, grocery bag, keys, lamp, heavy sculpture, coffee cup, rolled up magazine, hot coffee.
- o Whip your keys into his face. Notice that these keys are attached to a strap. The strap adds greater force to the whipping strike (5).
- o Throw hot coffee in his face (6).

SELF-DEFENSE IN THE NEWS

A 58-year-old woman fought off two men after they broke into her home. First, she threw a bowl of chili onto them and then commenced beating them with a broom. When she began throwing other household objects, they decided they had had enough and fled.

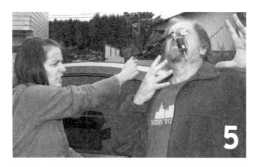

Flexible weapons

○ pants belt, scarf, rolled up jacket, rope.

○ Snap your pants belt into his face (7).

○ Whip your jacket into his face (8).

Compound weapons

○ Knife: stab with the point, cut with the length, hit with the butt); pointy ceramic: poke with the point and hit with the mass; belt (strangle with the length and hit with the buckle end.

○ Jab him with the pointy end of the ceramic and then slug him with it (9-11).

War story: Loren once had to arrest an extremely violent and mentally deranged man who had jump-kicked a preacher in the jaw in the middle of his sermon. Then the man climbed up into the church attic where he stripped nearly naked. After the he kicked the first responding officer in the face, Loren grabbed an old mattress lying in a corner, and charged toward the man, knocking him down and restraining him with it. Officers quickly applied restraints to his protruding hands and ankles.

PUSH HIM OVER AN OBJECT OR INTO AN OBJECT

When you're aware of your environment and quick to recognize a sidewalk curb, stair step, piece of furniture or countertop as more than what they were intended for, you're more apt to use them in the heat of the moment.

When pushing an attacker over a chair or tricking him into tripping over a curb, you change his focus from you to himself. Let's say that he is in your face threatening you with vile words and dangerous gestures. Maybe he slapped you or pushed you. All his thoughts are on you and the fear he wants to instill in your head. Then you push him over a stool (1). Just like that, his mind switches from you to himself, and where he is about to land and how much it might hurt (2). This gives you a second to pick up another environmental weapon or to flee the scene.

The You-know-what-really-hurts? Game

Some people might argue that this is a sick game. We don't deny that, but we also know that it's an easy way to learn to see common objects as potential weapons that might save our lives. Here is the game.

Your coworker is leaning over your cubicle wall. "You know what would really hurt?" she asks. "This stapler slammed against Mr. Johnson's forehead."

"You know what would really hurt?" you ask. "This copy machine thrown into my psycho ex-husband's groin."

Yes, it's a little sick, but it gets you thinking outside the parameters of what the object is designed for. You can even play the game by yourself.

You're walking to your car with a bag of groceries. You ask yourself: You know what would really hurt? This can of Hungry Man soup smashed into a mugger's cheek.

You're looking through your purse for something and you see your pen. You ask yourself: You know what would really hurt? This pen driven into the back of my blind date's wandering hand.

Try the game. You will never see everyday objects the same again.

USE ENVIRONMENTAL OBJECTS TO SLOW HIM DOWN

When Loren was a cop working the downtown precinct, he often stood so that there was a fire hydrant, parking meter or car fender between him and a volatile person. Because cops don't have the luxury of walking or running away from a dangerous person, Loren used these things as devices that would increase his response time should the person attack. To get to him, the attacker would have to move around the object, which gave Loren a second or two more to react.

Part of your awareness includes noting such opportunities when they arise.

- When your spouse is about to hit you, push him over a coffee table.

- When an aggressive street person turns belligerent because you refuse to give him money, step behind one of those heavy trashcans (1).

- When a drunk turns mean on you in a nightclub, push him over a barstool.

- When an angry motorist gets even angrier, step to the other side of your fender (2).

Sometimes fate literally hands you the opportunity when the attacker unintentionally stands with something directly behind him. Other times you have to maneuver him in front of something using subterfuge. Once he is where you want him, wait until he is distracted and then attack him with a hard shove.

What the police want to know

- The address of where the incident happened. If you don't know the exact address, tell them something like, "The big blue house on 47th, two houses in from Main." Or, "The unmarked building one block south of Shaver grade school."
- Describe the suspect's general appearance, including skin color, height, age, body type and hair color.
- Describe what the suspect wore, to include colors and specific styles.
- Describe tattoos, scars, glasses and facial hair.
- Make, model and color of the car. Use names to help you remember a license plate. For example, ABC123 would be Alice, Beth, Claire 1, 2, 3.
- Write everything down as soon as possible.
- You might recall additional information 24 to 48 hours after a traumatic event. Call the police and provide them with it.

USE THE ATTACKER'S CLOTHING

Use the attacker's clothing as an improvised weapon. We call the next two techniques "ghost hits" because the attacker can't see what is hitting him.

GHOST HIT 1

An attacker wearing a baseball hat grabs at you as you leave your home (1). Reach up and cup the back of his head with one hand (2) and push the bill of his hat over his eyes with your other (3).

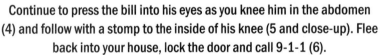

Continue to press the bill into his eyes as you knee him in the abdomen (4) and follow with a stomp to the inside of his knee (5 and close-up). Flee back into your house, lock the door and call 9-1-1 (6).

Once inside, retrieve something to use as a weapon in case he breaks in. If he leaves, watch through the window where he goes so you can inform the police.

To reiterate, consider everything around you a potential weapon or something that you can use to help your situation. We heard of a woman who threw her cat into an attacker's face.

GHOST HIT 2

The attacker has forced you down onto a sofa. Grab a wad of the lower section of his jacket...

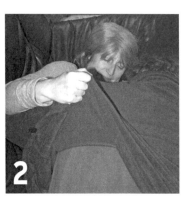

...and pull it up...

...and over his head. Now it's all about choices.

You can extract your hand and hammerfist...

...his head. Or you can lift your right knee...

...to bump him off you...

...and onto to the floor.

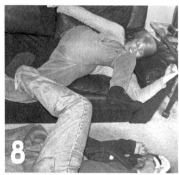

Then kick him.

This is our desk. We're armed with a stapler, pens, steel coffee mug, CD cases, cell phone, three computer screens, keyboard, lamp, and a three-ring binder. To the left, just outside of the photo, are scissors, more pens, steel hand grippers, heavy books, a pocketknife and a TV screen. Out of the pic to the right are heavy boxes of books, a stool, two 5-pound sleeping dogs (hey, they will be in the fight, too) and a printer. Behind us are more books, several box openers, a big knife, a heavy-duty tape dispenser and a paper shredder. Don't even get us started on the cache in the closet. We have enough weapons within reach that we could take over the neighborhood. What do you got around you right now?

How should a woman train?

There is no "wait and see" time if an attack is eminent. When your instincts tell you it's a go, you go girl.

■ ■ ■

Any kind of physical contact, be it a push, a grab, or a strike is cause to attack back.

■ ■ ■

Train on situations you've read about in the news.

■ ■ ■

I train on situations in which a person encroaches in my personal space. First, I will act verbally, make direct eye contact with him, and put my hands up to guard my space. I do this to let him know I'm aware of him and that I don't want him getting too close. If he brandishes a weapon or starts to put his hands on me, then it's time to defend aggressively.

■ ■ ■

Women have been attacked anywhere and everywhere. So you should practice in your car, in your basement, in your laundry room, in a hallway. No scenarios are too extreme.

CHAPTER SIX

SCENARIOS

Let's look at an assortment of scenarios in a variety of locations using techniques from Chapters Two and Three. The scenarios are typical ones that Loren investigated as a police officer and typical of those you read about in the news. We suggest practicing a scenario as we show it here as many times as it takes for you to feel comfortable with it. Then add a slight variation. For example, if we picture the attacker grabbing with his right hand, change it so that he grabs you with his left. It's not a big change, but you will see quickly that it alters your response.

Don't be in a hurry to change. Do one method at least 20 times: do 1 set of 10 reps, rest for half a minute or so, and then practice a second set of 10 reps. If you don't feel comfortable yet, do more sets until you do. It might take you two or three training days before you're ready to modify the scenario, and that's fine. Don't change it because you're bored or because you're frustrated. Change it because you're comfortable with one method and you're ready for another. We talk more about training in Chapter Eight, "How to Practice."

SELF-DEFENSE IN THE NEWS

Just as a five-foot-tall, 115-pound woman got out of her car at a service station, a thief jumped in behind the wheel and attempted to steal it. The woman scrambled into the passenger side and fought to get her keys back. When she couldn't, she began screaming and punching him until he opened the door and fled. "It's the only thing I have to get to work," she said.

Practice calling 9-1-1

Practice calling 9-1-1!? There are only three numbers; I think I can handle that.

Maybe, but people under stress have had trouble. Know that when your heart rate is going *bumpbumpbump* at 200 beats a minute or higher, your ability to do any fine-motor skill is virtually nonexistent. In fact, it begins to deteriorate at 115 beats per minute. With an accelerated heart rate, you're likely to have a difficult time putting a key into a car ignition, writing down a license plate number, executing a complex self-defense technique, and calling 9-1-1.

Rehearse whatever skill you might have to do under stress ahead of time. If you dial 9-1-1 on a cell phone, you must remember to hit "send" at the end. If you're calling 9-1-1 in an office, you might need to dial 9 to get an outside line. You can easily do these things now when you're calm and collected, but when your heart is rattling in your ears like a machine gun, it's a different story. Rehearse these things two or three times a month so that they are there for you when you need them. Be sure to turn off the phone first.

While the woman in the Self-defense in the News on the previous page was successful, she was lucky. She gave up her place of relative safety (outside her car) and got inside a dangerous place to do battle with a felon. Not only could the small woman have been hurt at the service station, the thief could have driven her to a second crime scene to assault or kill her.

- Don't give up a strong position for one that is dangerous.

- Don't let emotion cause you to take dangerous risks.

- Don't put yourself in a position where you can be driven somewhere else.

- Don't get hurt or killed over property.

IN AND OUT OF CAR #1

You're behind the steering wheel when an attacker leaps in your passenger door (always keep it locked) and demands that you drive him somewhere.

When he is close enough, hit him multiple times...

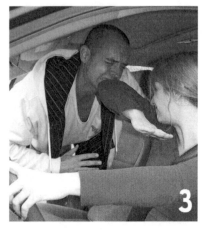

...with a side elbow to the face.

When he falls back or pulls away, hit him multiple times with a...

...side hammerfist.

Push him out or, after he falls out on his own, drive away. Don't worry about your open door until you're far enough away to close it.

IN AND OUT OF CAR #2

1

An attacker is trying to force you into his car.

2

Supporting yourself on the seat with your right arm, twist to the side, thrust your left hand into his face and rake...

3

...downward like a cat's scratching a post.

4

When he staggers back a step, chamber your side stomp kick...

5

...and thrust it into the closest target. Then flee.

IN AND OUT OF CAR #3

1

3

When he stumbles back and falls over a curb, get into your car, lock the doors and flee (3).

You're putting something in the trunk when a man steps close enough to touch you with his body (1). Drive a rear elbow into his midsection repeatedly (2).

He pushes you against a stove and (1) draws his hand back to punch (2) your face but you shield block it with your arm (3).

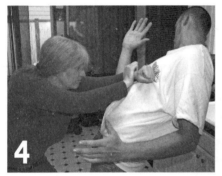

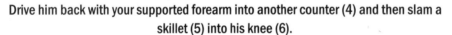

Drive him back with your supported forearm into another counter (4) and then slam a skillet (5) into his knee (6).

Shield Block

The shield block is a natural move that requires only quick reflexes. You see the strike coming and you snap your forearm up to cover the side of your face. Position your fist a little behind your ear and press your forearm against the side of your head. Don't hold your forearm away from your head because that causes you to get hit twice, once when the blow hits your arm and again when your arm hits your skull.

Does it hurt to get hit in the arm? Yes. Is it better than being punched in the skull? Yes.

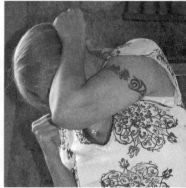

IN THE HOME #2

He grabs your head and yanks it downward (1). Before you're too far off balance, kick his shin two or three times. If you can get away at this point, do so. If you can't and he escalates the force, you must stop him before he hurts you (2). While he is still reacting to his hurt leg, rip your claws down and over (3)...

...his nipple (4). If you can, rip it again with your other hand. Both claws are fast a furious (5). Follow without hesitation an elbow slam (6) into the side of his neck (7).

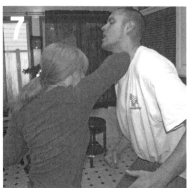

SELF-DEFENSE IN THE NEWS

A judge found that a woman acted in self-defense when she struck her husband in the head with a toilet tank lid. She told the judge during the trial that she "knew what was coming" when he forced her into the bathroom.

Never hit an attacker and then watch what happens. Even veteran martial artists know that it often takes more than one hit to take an opponent out of the fight—and these guys hit hard! An attacker just might eat your single blow like a tasty snack and then attack you with even greater intensity. When you have the right to hit in self-defense, keep hitting until the attacker is unable to continue, he flees, or an avenue of escape opens for you to flee. If the first target you hit remains open, hit it again. If it is no longer open, hit a different one. And another after that.

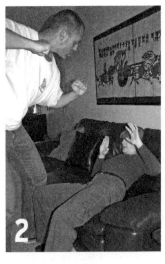

3 Before he hits you, snap your shin up and into his groin two times, three if possible.

Your partner pushes you down onto a sofa.

He bends toward you shouting, threatening.

Then chamber your leg to...

...kick or shove him back...

...so you can get away.

Pepper spray

Pepper spray contains an active ingredient called OC (Oleoresin Capsicum) and other inert ingredients. When sprayed into the mucous membranes—eyes, nose, throat, and lungs—the recipient suffers temporary blindness, difficulty breathing, extreme tearing and mucous flow. The effects of the pepper spray last between 20 and 90 minutes, giving you plenty of time to escape your terrifying situation.

Contrary to what manufacturers and retail outlets tell you, pepper spray does not work on everyone. "It has no effect on 3 out of 10 people," one police veteran told us.

If you decide to carry it, learn how to use it. There are plenty of free instructional videos on-line and most products come with written instructions. As with all techniques in this book, spray the attacker and then flee when he reacts. Don't stick around to enjoy your work.

IN THE HOME #4

1 Your partner says he is going to make you pay and then angrily yanks your arm until...

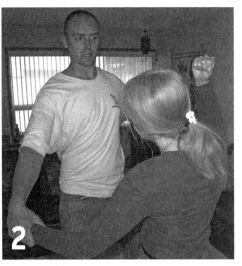

2 ...you're standing. You know from the past that he intends to hit you. Don't wait. Repeatedly slam a powerful...

3 ...hammerfist down onto the beefy part of his forearm near his elbow.

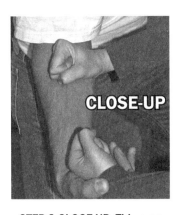

CLOSE-UP

STEP 3 CLOSE UP: This area is tender and repeated blows can numb his hand and make it difficult for him to continue holding on.

4 Assume he maintains his grip. Know that when he is holding you, he limits the use of his hand. So when he draws his other one back to hit you, step in the direction of his occupied hand. If he does manage to hit you, the awkwardness of his position diminishes his power a little. In addition, since your free arm is already up, you can easily shield block it.

5

CLOSE-UP

Whip a powerful slap into his throat. A blow to the Adam's apple is highly effective, though dangerous. Be justified.

SELF-DEFENSE IN THE NEWS

A UK woman named Carr went to the defense of her girlfriend whose husband of three weeks was assaulting her. Drunk and enraged, the man punched Carr, knocking her to the ground and then sat on her to hold her down. Carr took advantage of target availability and bit one of the newlywed's testicles...off (it was later found but the doctors were unable to reattach). In an unbelievable departure from common sense, the courts charged Carr with assault and sentenced her to six months in jail.

You're unable to block his slap (1) which knocks you back into a corner, trapped and unable to escape (2). When he draws his hand back to hit you, spring like a lioness and rip your angry claws (3)....

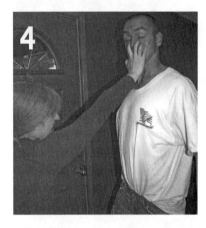

...down his face (4). Follow immediately with your other hand. Rip it (5)...

...down his face (6). If needed, do another with the first hand (7). Break out of the corner as soon as you're able, and flee.

Claw fast and furious. There is no pause between your left claw and your right. The instant one hand reaches the bottom of the claw motion, the other hand starts at the top. Don't think: *Claw. Then claw. Then another claw.* Instead, think: *Clawclawclaw.*

IN THE HOME #6

A man pulls you down onto the floor and onto him. You can't squirm out of his strength and you can't hit because your arms are pinned.

But you can bite him. Where? Anywhere. Teeth hurt whatever and wherever they chomp. For example, his cheek or...

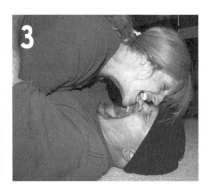

...his nose.

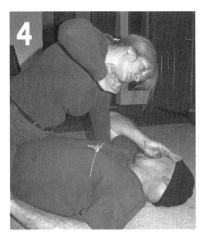

STEP 3 OPTIONS: You can: 1) bite him multiple times as if chomping a corn on the cob; 2) bite deeply into him and then pull your head back with his flesh still in your mouth; or 3) bite into him and then shake your head back and forth like a dog with a chew toy.

When he releases his grip on your arms—and he will—use the best weapon to continue your attack, your elbow in this case (4). Hit repeatedly until you can push off him and flee (5).

OUTSIDE #1

For instructional purposes, Lisa stops jogging when approached. Normally, you would keep running should someone step out from behind a tree. However, it's also possible you stopped for a drink of water or to tie a shoelace.

You're out jogging (1) when a man approaches. Put up your hands and shout loudly, "Stay back! Don't come closer (2)." Some rapists have said that they will back off when a woman demonstrates that she will not be an easy target. Run off (3) and call 9-1-1 (4) as soon as you can do so safely. Provide them with a description of the subject and where you saw him. Don't be reluctant to call. The police will check him out and write a small report on their contact. They will match his info against any past incidents in the area and against any that happen in the future.

OUTSIDE #2

You're unable to flee and El Creepo rushes you.

From your leave-me-alone stance, switch mentally and physically into your attack mode as he...

...lunges for you. Knock aside his arm ...

...and slam a diagonally hammerfist...

...into the side of his head or ear.

Take advantage of his pain up high...

... to give him some down low, with a shin kick to his groin. Then flee.

SELF-DEFENSE IN THE NEWS

One late night, an attacker grabbed a 23-year-old woman who was out walking and listening to her iPod. He dragged her into a park where he straddled her and threatened her with a box cutter. He told her twice that he was going to rape and kill her. The woman knew that she was, in her words, "In a kill or be killed situation." She said she had "absolutely nothing to lose." She yelled that she was going to kill him first and began scratching his eyes and face with her nails. He got off her and fled.

Although the woman in the news item might not have had a choice about walking on a street late at night, she did have a choice about listening to her iPod. She might have heard the attacker approaching if she had not been listening to music. Or he might not have chosen her if she hadn't been so obviously distracted. However, her decision to attack him was a good one. She said later that she remembers her self-defense instructor saying that rapists like to follow a "rape script," a fantasy of how they want the situation to play out. When the victim acts outside the script—she fights back—she undermines the attacker's sense of control.

Should he not react to your blows…

Pick up something to use as a weapon, a rock in this case, and...

... smack him in the groin with it.

Then deliver another blow up high...

...into his forehead.

Jogging safety tips

- Jog with a friend.

- Jog in an area with which you are familiar.

- Don't jog in an out-of-the-way area.

- Jog during daylight hours only.

- Jog facing oncoming traffic.

- If followed, go to the nearest house and call the police.

- Carry a cell phone.

- Wear bright colored clothing.

- Carry pepper spray.

- Vary your running course and how you run it.

- Be alert and aware of your surroundings.

- Don't listen to an iPod-like device.

- Keep away from bushes and trees where an attacker might be waiting.

- Know that not all male joggers are running for legit reasons

GRABS

Every self-defense class teaches defenses against grabs, moves that are often called escapes. Some defenses are so insanely complicated that most people forget them in a real situation, some work only for people built like Ms. Universe but not for us average folks, and some are just wishful thinking, meaning they work okay in training but not in the means streets.

We are not against all escape techniques, but for our purposes here, we think it's best to keep things simple. Therefore, we use the same techniques toddlers use. When a three-year-old boy grabs a three-year-old girl's arm, she doesn't spin to her right, duck to her left and a do triple ballet pirouette, as some self-defense classes teach as a way to escape. She keeps it simple: She clobbers the little dude. And that is what you can do, too.

The idea is to hit a vulnerable target so the grabber gets distracted from his grip. The human brain can think of only one thing at a time. When you slam a hammerfist into his nose three times in rapid succession, his mind is going to be on the searing pain, his inability to breathe, and the heavy tearing that virtually blinds him. It won't be on his grab.

We are not talking about a mediocre hit but rather a savage and unrelenting assault on his body. Every woman we interviewed for this book said that an unasked for grab was her trigger to attack. He grabs and you hit him like a jackhammer on steroids.

ATTACKER GRABS YOUR SHIRT

Don't attempt a fancy hand-removal technique. Instead, grab his wrist to solidify his arm (so all of your blow's energy penetrates his limb) and then...

...hammerfist his upper forearm, just below the bend. Hit it several times.

Then slam a hammerfist, or several, into his face until he releases you.

ATTACKER GRABS YOUR ARM

Don't hesitate to see why he is grabbing you; it might be too late by the time you figure it out. Instantaneously...

... kick his shin several times. When he bends forward in pain...

...forearm smash his neck, chin, mouth, or nose.

CLOSE-UP

ATTACKER GRABS BOTH OF YOUR WRISTS (FRONT)

By grabbing both wrists, he has inadvertently tied up both of his hands. Take advantage of this and slam your shin into his groin.

Then kick his shin.

Then kick his groin again. Then kick his shin once more. Think: shingroinshingroinshin... You're a machine gun.

ATTACKER GRABS BOTH WRISTS FROM BEHIND

The instant you're grabbed,

Twist your body a little and side stomp kick...

...his thigh, knee or shin.

Then stomp...

...his foot.

After you feel comfortable with these simple, yet common scenarios, create your own. Start by combining parts of various techniques that we present here or create new ones. If you're concerned about an issue specific to your lifestyle, then create scenarios that are applicable to your specific needs. Never rule out any possibility. Never say, "That would never happen." No matter how bizarre it might seem to you, it has occurred somewhere before and it will happen again.

How important is fitness in self-defense?

It's all important. Would you rather have an out of shape, overweight woman protect you or one that is in condition, strong and confident? You would of course want the fit one. What if the only person available to protect you—was you?

■ ■ ■

I think that many women battle with the issue of strength and its perceptions. While we admire strong women and hope to learn techniques that will keep us from being victimized, there is also a stigma associated with strength. Women are afraid to be labeled "battle-axes," "hard-asses," or "dykes." It is almost as if you can't be strong, independent, and powerful and still be feminine, nurturing, gentle or beautiful. It is ridiculous, but that underlying stereotype is very prevalent in our society.

■ ■ ■

Women need fitness and strength.

■ ■ ■

Most women who have trained for any length of time have been up against someone who was bigger, stronger, or more intimidating. Being fit and strong, which extends to all of your techniques, gives you the edge.

■ ■ ■

So many women think that they are going to get unsightly muscle if they train to get strong. Not true. What they will get is stronger, improved fitness, and power to enhance their self-defense techniques.

CHAPTER SEVEN

"GETTING STRONG NOW"

Hey, get back here! Don't skip this chapter. We're not going to lecture you on fitness and diet. Not because they aren't important, because they are; in fact, they are absolutely critical. But we would be remiss if we didn't talk about strength a little and give you three exercises that you will like doing, that is, when you're done hating them.

If you're a big exerciser now, you already know how good being fit feels and the confidence it gives you. If you don't train, we strongly encourage you to try the following three exercises for a few weeks. We think you will enjoy the benefits so much that you will want to make them part of your lifestyle. For sure, you will see a huge improvement in the speed and power you can deliver in all your self-defense techniques.

Consider these simple factoids: Being strong and fit:

- means you have a better chance of surviving an attack.
- makes you feel more confident
- makes you less of a target.
- translates to greater power and speed.
- can reduce the chance of you getting hurt.
- feels good.

3 Exercises for Speed and Power

The following three exercises are done freehand, meaning that you don't need equipment other than your creaking bones and sweaty brow. It's a simple routine that isn't about screaming, grunting and all the other nonsense that goes on in health clubs. It's about one thing: getting stronger.

The exercises work three sections of your body: 1) your torso and arms, 2) your center, also known as the core, 3) and your lower body, your butt and legs.

UPPER BODY AND ARMS

The muscles of your upper body, to include your chest, back, shoulders, and the muscles of your arms, especially your triceps, are all involved in pushing someone away, pushing yourself up from the ground, and striking with your palm-heels, fists, forearms and elbows. Greater strength means greater stopping power.

THE CORE

Every modern fitness program now includes, even emphasizes, exercises to develop the core. The muscles of your center, to include your abdomen, sides and lower back are involved in all offensive and defensive moments. When the core muscles are fit and strong, you enjoy more power, flexibility and speed, critical attributes for survival.

LOWER BODY

Your legs and rear together create a formidable powerhouse to launch devastating kicks, pushes, pulls, palm-heel strikes and forearm smashes. The stronger your lower half, the more able you are to withstand being pushed, pulled or knocked off balance.

You don't have to block out 90 minutes per workout day, you don't have to go to an expensive gym or buy little exercise outfits (okay, if buying an exercise outfits helps, go ahead.) All you need is about 15 minutes, twice a week. Space your workouts so there are one or two rest days between them.

Let's say you've been porking out all weekend and you feel like a slug. Can you train three days this coming week? Sure, if it makes you feel better body-wise and conscience-wise. But normally, two days a week is all you need. What if something comes up and you can only train once in a seven-day period? In the beginning, skipping workouts is not a good idea because it will slow your progress or stop it. During the first two months, make every effort to do your exercises twice a week. After that, if occasionally you can only get in one session, it's not so bad, though you should make that session a hard one.

Note: Your goal is to get into a habit of doing your 15-minute session twice a week. When you start missing workouts, your brain plays tricks on you. It will convince you that missing training is okay, that you need extra rest, that you need to bake a cake, or that you need to visit a friend. In short order, you develop a new habit, one of not exercising.

SUCCESS STORY 1:

Loren recently strained a shoulder muscle while training on a heavy punching bag. After recuperating for a few days, he found that the pain prevented him from doing even one pushup on the balls of his feet, but he could do five on his knees. A week later, he could do seven, then 10, and then 15. Within a few weeks, he was once again doing multiple sets and reps on the balls of his feet.

SUCCESS STORY 2:

A middle-aged and slightly overweight woman who works with Lisa decided to start a pushup routine. Her goal was to do 15 on the balls of her feet but she quickly discovered that she could not do a single, lonesome pushup. Lisa suggested that she get on her hands and knees and slowly lower herself to the floor using muscle power to control the pace. She could use whatever method she wanted to get back up, but she had to lower herself slowly and with control. She could do 5 slow-lowering reps the first week, but within two weeks she could do 7, and at the three-week mark she could do 10 slow-lowering reps. Within a month she could do 2 complete up-and-down reps on her knees; two weeks later she could do 7. Two months after she began her program, she could do two pushups on the balls of her feet. She is still progressing.

Pushups

Let's dispel that old wife's tale that if you do pushups on the balls of your feet (aka: men's pushups) your ovaries will pop loose and roll across the floor. While this myth still haunts the Internet—It. Ain't. Gonna. Happen. Lisa can do 9 sets of 15 reps each of so-called 'men's pushups" and everything is just fine, thank you very much.

Let's start by discarding the terms men's pushups and women's pushups, and replacing them with beginner's pushups and on-the-balls-of your-feet pushups. If you lack upper body strength or you're recovering from an injury, doing pushups on your knees is the fastest way to build the foundation strength needed to do pushups on the balls of your feet.

WHAT THEY ARE GOOD FOR

The pushup lets you know immediately your fitness and strength level. The simple act of pushing yourself up engages muscle groups in your arms, chest, back, abdomen, hips and legs. "It takes strength to do them, and it takes endurance to do a lot of them," said the late Jack LaLanne, the fitness guru who shocked television viewers in the '50s by doing fingertip pushups (not recommended, by the way) and later setting a world record by doing 1,033 pushups in 23 minutes. "It's a good indication of what kind of physical condition you're in."

At the risk of being overdramatic, strength gained through pushups could be the deciding factor in a self-defense situation. Such as:

- pushing yourself up when an attacker is lying on your back.

- pushing an attacker off you when he is lying on your front.

- pushing an attacker away when you're both standing.

- pushing a heavy chair or table into an advancing attacker.

- holding a door closed when an attacker is trying to force his way in.

- executing any type of straight-line push, palm-heel, elbow strike, and forearm strike.

Keep in mind that you're exercising, not trying to set a world record, not trying to one-up your partner, and not trying to max out each workout. Your goal is to progress, and that's all. Remembering that goes a long way toward keeping you injury free and making gains.

If you can already do pushups on the balls of your feet, jump ahead to that section. If you can do knee pushups, jump to that section. If you need help doing knee pushups, stay right here.

WALL PUSHUPS

This is a good way to get started doing pushups because most of the weight is on your feet, not your arms.

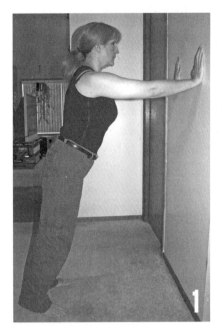  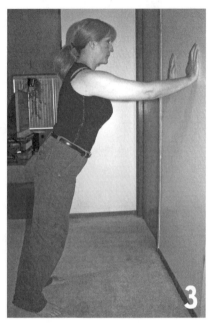

Stand about 3 feet away from the wall, lean in and place your palms on the wall, shoulder width apart.

When you can do 3 sets of 10-15 reps with a minute rest between sets, you're ready for knee pushups.

Lower your body until your nose is half an inch from the wall and your forearms are flush with it. If you cannot go that far, go as far as you can. Keep at it and in 2 or 3 weeks you'll go all the way down.

Push back until your arms are almost straight, about an inch short. Don't lock out your elbows as that can hurt them. Strive for an even rhythm down and up for as many repetitions as you can. Try for 10.

KNEE PUSHUPS: FEET UP

If you don't need to condition yourself on the wall, start with these. We show you two ways to make knee pushups progressively harder to build strength for doing pushups on the balls of your feet. However, there is no rush to reach that goal. It's called progressive exercise for a reason: It's safe and it works.

Get down on your all fours. Place your hands about shoulder width apart to duplicate the path of the palm-heel strike. Placing them wider can cause shoulder strain. Raise your feet to make the pushup a little easier (1). Keep your body as straight as an arrow and lower yourself down until your chest touches the floor (2). Push yourself back up until your arms are straight. Again, don't lock your elbows (3). When you can do 3 sets of 10-15 reps—it might take a month or two—move on to the next variation.

KNEE PUSHUPS: FEET DOWN

Get onto your hands and knees and lower your feet until they are on the floor. This places a little more workload on your arms and a lot more on your core, your center.

Keep your body as straight as an arrow and lower yourself down until the front of your body touches the floor.

Push yourself back up. When you can do 3 sets of 10-15 reps— it might take a month or two—move on to the next variation.

How to Think

No matter what variation of pushup you're doing, it's important that you mentally "see" the move as a fighting technique. See the upward thrust as a punch or a push. Verbalize the action on each count as you push upward: "Punch one," "Punch two..." Or, "Push one" "Push two..." This helps you stay focused and helps you think of the exercise as a self-defense movement.

PUSHUPS: BALLS OF YOUR FEET

If you're a veteran of doing pushups on the balls of your feet and you're starting with this section, good for you. If you had to progress through the other variations to reach this one, congrats, you made it.

Arms and hands under your shoulders, feet together and on the balls. Imagine that you're a wooden plank. Wooden planks don't sag in the middle or stick their butts up in the air. They remain straight.

Lower your body until your chest and chin touch the floor.

Push yourself back up without locking out your elbows. Work until you can do 3 sets of 10-15 reps comfortably.

You can remain at 3 sets of 10-15 reps or you can add one or two more sets and increase the reps to 20. You can also seek out ways to make pushups on the balls of your feet more difficult. We once had a class of 30 students think up 30 different ways of doing pushups. On the next page are a few more that we like.

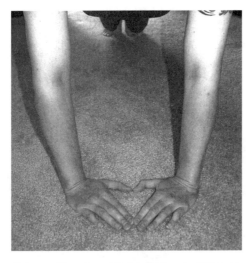

Put your thumb and index fingers together to form the shape of a spade. This emphasizes the backs of your arms.

Uneven pushups stimulate progress by confusing your muscles. Take turns so that you do the same number with each hand on the raised surface.

Place your feet on something so they are higher than your hands. This increases the weight on your arms and upper chest.

Lift one leg to increase the weight on your arms and work your core a little harder. Alternate legs.

Don't worry. You're not going to add bulky muscles. However, you will add formidable power to your upper body.

Lisa progressively—over two to three months—works up to 9 sets of 15 reps of pushups. So that she doesn't get stale, she takes a break from them and works her way up to 4 sets of 15 reps with a 25-pound weight on her back. This too takes two to three months. Then she takes a break from that and returns to working up to 9 sets of 15 reps again. Do *you* have to do this? Not at all. She just likes to push herself.

Core

From golf to swimming to volleyball to bodybuilding, the mantra of the new millennium is "You gotta work your core muscles." People training for self-defense are no exception. In fact, to reach your full potential, strengthening the core is all-important.

Core muscles refer to those in and around your torso, excluding your arms, legs and head. Specifically, most trainers consider the core to be those muscles in your abdomen, sides, and in your mid and lower back.

They come into play when you punch, kick, grapple, jump, and get up quickly from the floor. You even use them when standing there deciding whether to fight or turn and run. The stronger your core, the better you will be at these movements.

Here are two progressive exercises that strengthen your core (and flatten your tummy, too). If you're familiar with the front plank and can already do it on the balls of your feet, jump to that section. If you're new to these exercises, we strongly suggest that you do them on your knees for two or three weeks. This will condition your core for doing them on the balls of your feet without making you sore.

FRONT PLANK ON YOUR KNEES

Another reminder: You're exercising to build strength; you're not trying to prove anything to anyone. Start out slowly and build up progressively.

Get down onto the floor and rest on your knees and forearms. Your elbows should be right under your shoulders. Keep your back straight so that you're not sagging and your rear isn't sticking up.

1. Hold this position for 20 seconds, then lie down and rest for 30 seconds.

2. Then repeat for another 20 seconds.

3. Rest a day.

4. The following day, repeat the 2 sets. If you can add 5 seconds to each set, do so.

Continue with this pattern until you can do 2 sets, 60 seconds each. This might take you several weeks to achieve. Don't force it; enjoy the process.

FRONT PLANK ON THE BALLS OF YOUR FEET

When you have completed 2 sets of 60 seconds each on your knees for three or four weeks, you're ready for the next step. Or if you've done core work before and you're in good shape, you can jump right into this tougher variation.

Get down onto the floor and rest on your forearms and the balls of your feet. Since this is a lot tougher, start over at 20 seconds. If that is too easy, increase the time a few seconds on your second set. Your goal is 2 sets of 60 seconds each. Once you've reached this goal—it might take two to three months—you can continue to do the two sets and enjoy the strength you've built in your core or you can make the exercise tougher with the following variations.

FRONT PLANK, LEG LIFT

This really adds stress on your core while working the ol' butt muscles at the same time. Strong glutes are good for kicking, strong stances and tight jeans.

You're going to do a 60-second plank with two leg lifts within the minute.

1. Get onto your forearms and the balls of your feet and lift your right leg a few inches off the floor.

2. Hold it there for 20 seconds, put it down and then lift your left leg for 20 seconds.

3. Set that leg down and, with both feet on the floor, continue with your plank for 20 more seconds. That completes your first 60-second set.

4. Rest for 30 seconds and then do another set, repeating the procedure for 60 seconds.

If 20 seconds is too long, simply reduce the time to, say, 10 seconds with each leg and then finish the set on both feet for 40 seconds. Over the weeks, progressively increase the time that you hold up your legs. Most trainees strive to hold one leg up for 30 seconds and then hold the other leg up for 30 seconds. Then they lower themselves all the way down to rest for 30 to 60 seconds. Then they do the second set the same way.

To really test your strength (and build buns of iron), hold your left leg up for the entire first 60-second set, rest for 30 and then hold your right leg up for the entire second set.

Want an even tougher version? You're an animal!

This time add a kick to your plank. This challenges and strengthens your rear and all the other muscles in your legs and core.

KICKING FROM THE PLANK

Get on your forearms and the balls of your feet, draw your knee in...

...and thrust your foot back. Hold it out for two seconds and then retract. Then do another kick. Do 5 kicks with your left leg and then 5 with your right, all within the 60-second set. After completing the first set, rest for 30 seconds and then repeat the same number of kicks in the second 60-second set.

SIDE PLANK

This tough exercise targets your sides and lower back, important muscles that help you twist away from someone, slam home a palm-heel strike, get up from the ground quickly, and throw that hard-hitting kick.

If you have done this exercise before and you can handle the on-your-feet position, jump ahead to that section. If you're new to this, we suggest you start on your knees for two or three weeks and then try the on-your-feet version.

ON YOUR KNEES

Get down on your side and rest on your forearm, which should be directly under your shoulder, with your legs bent so that your lower body rests on your knees.

Lift your side off the floor as high as you can and hold for 20 seconds. Rest and then repeat for another set of 20. When you can do 2 sets of 60 seconds each, you're ready to progress to the next variation.

ON YOUR FEET

Rest on your forearm, which is directly under your shoulder, extend your legs straight and off the floor, and stack your feet. Do 2, 20-second sets on each side. When you can do 2 sets, 60 seconds on each side, you're ready to progress to the next stage.

Don't let your side droop. Imagine something passing underneath you, such as a slithering, poisonous snake, and suck your side up accordingly.

SIDE PLANK WITH REACH

This is harder than it looks but oh so good for you. It develops extraordinary power in your core.

Assume the side plank and extend your arm over your head.

Slowly, lower your hand under your abdomen and reach toward your far side. Your hips might lift a little, which is fine.

Return to the hand-up position. Instead of watching the clock, count your reaches. Start with 2 sets of 5 reps on each side. Strive for 2 sets of 25 reps on each side.

Squats

Your legs are arguably the strongest muscle groups in your body. It's said in boxing that "a fighter is only as good as his legs"—and boxers don't kick! However, their legs are in constant motion as they stalk, retreat, advance, and circle. They also help stabilize the fighter when he is clinching and when he is absorbing punishment.

Your legs keep you upright to evade, push, pull, lunge, strike, kick, knee, and then run when you have the opportunity. At any given moment, you, like a boxer, are only as good as your legs.

Let's look at bodyweight squats. They are easy to do but believe this: You will be grunting and cursing us. But in three months, you will want to send us small gifts, so happy you will be over your results (chocolate is always nice to receive). Your goal with any of the variations is 3 sets of 35 reps. Yes, 35 per set.

BODYWEIGHT SQUATS

Stand with your heels (heels, not toes) shoulder width apart, your feet angled outward slightly, and your hands in front of your body about groin high. Look straight ahead throughout the exercise (1). Push your butt back a little as if you're about to sit in a chair and raise your arms until your hands are in front of your belly button (2). As you bend your knees and raise your arms, feel your bodyweight shift to your heels so (3) ...

... you can tap your toes, which indicates that your weight is properly on your heels. Raise your arms to face-high. This helps your balance and keeps your chest high. Your rear should be a little lower than your knees (4). Push yourself back up, reversing the action of your arms, until you're once again (5) standing (6).

Squatting this low is an advanced position. See the next section for an alternative.

VARIATION:

If you have bad knees or you have not exercised your legs in a long while, don't squat as low as just shown. Instead, lower yourself to one of the following positions:

BEGINNING AND INTERMEDIATE POSITIONS:

Lower yourself only one third of the way down and then push back up to the standing position. Do it this way for 3 to 6 weeks.

When you feel you're ready, lower yourself half way down until your thighs are horizontal with the floor, and then push back up to the standing position. Continue squatting to this depth for a few weeks before you progress to going all the way down.

If you never want to squat all the way, no problem. Just lower yourself one third or half of the way. You will still increase your leg strength.

How to progress with squats:

- Whether you can go all the way or part way, begin with 3 sets of 8-10 reps with a full 60-second rest in between. If you need 2 minutes, that is okay.

- Add 1 to 5 reps every other workout session. If there are workouts when you don't feel you can increase your reps, don't. Stay at your current number until your mind and body says you can add more.

- Continue to add reps until you can do 3 sets of 35 reps. Understand that this might take you three or four months. Also, understand that there is no rush. Increase at your pace and enjoy the progress you're making.

- If you have been doing:

  o one third squats and you have reached 3 sets of 35, you're ready to lower yourself to the one half squat position.

  o if you have been doing half squats, you're ready to do the advanced ones, in which you go all the way down.

- When you first try the new depth, reduce your reps from 3 sets of 35 to 3 sets of 15 reps. If that is too much, drop the rep count to 10 reps per set. If too little, increase it 20 reps per set.

TOUGHER BODYWEIGHT SQUATS

When you've reached your goal of 3 sets of 35, you can either maintain that count or you can kick it up a notch. Here is one way to make it more intense. We call them one and one half reps. They are hard so watch your language when the kids are around.

1 Assume the same starting position as before.

2 Squat all the way down.

3 Raise half way up...

4 ...and then go all the way back down again.

5 Then all the way back up to the starting position.

All that is one, single, solitary, lonely rep. Hello thigh burn!

If you have been doing 3 sets of 35 reps of regular down-and-up squats, reduce the rep count to, say, 20 reps per set until you get a sense of how your legs react to this harder squat version. If 20 reps are okay, slowly and progressively increase them until you're again doing 3 sets of 35 reps per set.

If 20 reps are too many, reduce the number to 10 or 15 for 3 sets and work on increasing them to 35.

Another way to increase reps

This pertains to all three exercises: pushups, braces and squats. Besides increasing reps in all sets simultaneously, you can also increase reps one set at a time.

For example, say you're doing 3 sets of 10 reps of squats.

- On your next workout, do 11 reps on set 1, and 10 reps on sets 2 and 3.

- The next workout, do 11 reps on sets 1 and 2, and 10 on set 3.

- On your next workout, do 11 reps on all three sets.

- Continue adding a rep per set in this fashion until you reach your goal.

A Workout

Here is a twice-a-week routine (in the next chapter we talk about combining workouts). Make sure there are two days of rest between each session. Follow this approach no matter what level you are. If you're a beginner, do fewer reps and hold postures for less time. If you're advanced, do the max.

PUSHUPS

3 sets, 15 reps of any variation you choose. If you can only do 3 sets of 3 reps at first, no problem. Keep at it until you reach 3 sets of 15 reps.

CORE

2 sets, 60 seconds each of any variation you choose. If you can only do 2 sets of 15 seconds at first, no problem. Keep at it until you can do 2 sets of 60 seconds.

SQUATS

3 sets of 35 reps of any variation you choose. If you can only do 3 sets of 5 reps at first, no problem. Keep at it until you reach 3 sets of 35 reps.

Rest 1 minute between each set and 3 minutes between each exercise. The entire routine will take less than 20 minutes.

Put on your favorite tunes and get to it.

How important is mindset in training?

I try to bring a feeling of empowerment to the participants in my classes. When threatened, I want them to think: "You may be attacking me, but you WILL regret it, and I will NOT go down without one hell of a fight."

■ ■ ■

In working with women who have been battered or otherwise victimized, I teach them to say to themselves: "I am worth fighting for, I deserve to live a long and happy life" or whatever else helps them to get through an attack. It gives the mind something to focus on, and sets the scene, if you will, for her response. This type of thinking should be used every time you train.

■ ■ ■

Bring to your training session, whether it's with a partner or by yourself, the determination not to be a victim. It might help your motivation to think that someone is attacking your child.

■ ■ ■

I love teaching with focus pads, kicking shields, and heavy bags; I believe these items really build mental focus, technical skill and physical strength.

■ ■ ■

Trust me, it's awful to be in the middle of an attack and think: I wish I would have practiced more.

■ ■ ■

What keeps me training is knowing that there are predators out there who would hurt me or my family and not think a thing about it.

CHAPTER EIGHT

HOW TO PRACTICE

It's not enough to learn self-defense techniques from a book, DVD or an instructor; you have to practice them, too. The more you do it, the more the movements ingrain into your memory and muscles. Practicing the techniques in this book is a win-win deal because you benefit in so many ways. Such as:

- The techniques become increasingly familiar, eventually becoming your go-to moves when you need them.

- Your muscles grow stronger and flexible, and your balance becomes sounder.

- As your skill level increases so does your confidence.

- You might drop a few pounds. *Really!?* It's true. Read on.

- You develop a powerful mindset that you're not going to be a victim, that you *will* fight back.

    Let's look at training frequency.

TRAINING ONCE A WEEK

Training one time a week is not as effective as training two times a week. Your muscles will not benefit as much because the ingraining process into your muscle memory will be minimal at best. If you miss a workout, it means you didn't train at all that week.

TRAINING TWO TO THREE TIMES A WEEK

In the beginning, training three times a week with a day off in between, such as Monday, Wednesday and Friday, optimally conditions your muscles and ingrain the techniques into your memory. If after two or three months you find that the time commitment is difficult for you, you can reduce your training to twice a week and still progress. We discuss combining your technique training with your twice weekly pushups, core and squats below.

Lisa practices martial arts three times a week and resistance exercises twice a week. Loren trains with resistance exercises four times a week (each muscle group only twice), and trains in the martial arts three to four times a week. Our students' routines are as varied as ours are. It's important to find one that fits with your lifestyle, one that you know that you can and will stay with.

For the first few weeks, we suggest that you practice the individual techniques in this book using the repetitions and sets we suggest in a moment. Your goal is to learn how to properly do the movements and understand how to apply them in a variety of situations.

Think of the repetitions as rubbing a block of wood with sandpaper. Each stroke smoothes the wood just a little. Do 10 strokes and the wood is smoother than it was before you began sanding. Do 3 sets of 10 swipes, and that wood changes even more. Do it two or three times a week and within a month or two, depending on how rough the wood was when you began, that wood will be as smooth as a baby's behind. The same holds true when practicing your self-defense techniques. The more reps you do, the smoother they become and the more deeply they imbed into your memory.

"The least you need to know" techniques

There are many ways to formulate a training session. Our first example uses the seven techniques from Chapter Three, "The least you need to know." Before you begin, reread the chapter so that you're familiar with all the angles we demonstrate.

The terms "side," "both sides, and "the other side" refer to your stance and the leg you have forward. For example, after completing 10 reps on your left side, left leg forward, you switch to your right side and do 10 reps with your right leg forward.

HAMMERFIST

There are four angles: vertical, diagonal, horizontal, and upward. Choose one angle to work each session and perform 3 sets of 10 repetitions on each side. Say you choose the vertical hammerfist.

Set 1: Stand left foot forward in your leave-me-alone stance. Using your rear, right hand, strike downward from 12 o'clock to 6 o'clock, stopping at about chest level. Do 10 reps.

Change sides and execute the hammer strike with your left fist, right leg forward, from 12 o'clock to 6 o'clock. Do 10 reps.

When you have done 10 reps on both sides, you have completed 1 set. Do two more sets on both sides to total 30 reps with your right arm and 30 with your left.

CLAWS

There are four angles: vertical, diagonal, horizontal, and upward. Choose one angle each workout. As with the hammer, you have completed one set when you perform 10 reps with your right hand, left foot forward, and 10 reps with your left hand, right foot forward. Do 3 sets of 10 reps on each side.

PALM-HEEL STRIKES

There are three angles: Straight forward, diagonally upward and straight up. Choose one angle each workout. You have completed one set when you perform 10 reps with your right hand, left foot forward, and 10 reps with your left hand, right foot forward. Do 3 sets of 10 reps on each side

ELBOWS

There are four angles: up, down, side and back. Choose one angle and perform 3 sets of 10 repetitions on each side. You have completed one set when you perform 10 reps with your right hand, left foot forward, and 10 reps with your left hand, right foot forward. Do 3 sets of 10 reps on each side.

FRONT KICK

There are two heights: low, into the attacker's shin or thigh, and medium high, into his midsection. Can't kick medium high? Then kick low. Alternate kicking with the ball of your foot, as if wearing flexible shoes, and kicking with the toe of your foot, as if wearing sturdy shoes. Do 3 sets of 10 reps on each side.

SIDE STOMP KICK

There are two heights: low, into the attacker's shin or thigh, and medium high, into his midsection. Do 3 sets on both sides kicking low. On your next workout, do 3 sets at medium height. Can't kick medium high? Then do all the sets kicking low.

Never worry about what you can't do. Stress what you can do.

SHIN KICK TO GROIN

Using your lower shin as your impact weapon, kick no higher than your own groin. Do 3 sets of 10 reps on both sides.

Here is what the workout looks like all together. Follow the same format no matter what angle of a technique you choose to practice.

Hammerfist: 3 sets, 10 reps, each side

Claws: 3 sets, 10 reps, each side

Palm-heel strikes: 3 sets, 10 reps each side

Elbows: 3 sets, 10 reps, each side

Front kick: 3 sets, 10 reps, each side

Side stomp kick: 3 sets, 10 reps each side

Shin kick: 3 sets, 10 reps, each side

YOU DON'T WANT TO TRAIN AEROBICALLY

Then don't. For some, training aerobically is fun and they enjoy the benefits of improved endurance. However, if you're training in some other fashion for aerobic and fat-burning benefits and you prefer to stick with that, or you simply don't want to train aerobically, no problem. Simply perform the sets and reps as described and rest whenever you want.

Form

Doing a technique with good form means that every part of your body is in perfect alignment as prescribed for that move. We tell you to put your feet this way, hold your head that way, position your arms like so, and rotate your hips thusly not because it looks pretty, though sometimes it does, but rather to optimize the technique's balance, power, speed, explosiveness and effectiveness on the target.

Practice in front of a mirror. Check your form against the images in this book. You might even have someone compare you against Lisa's photos to get an objective opinion.

RESTING BETWEEN REPS AND SETS

If you're new to exercise, rest 30 seconds between each set and a couple minutes between each new technique. If you're doing front kicks, for example:

- Do 1 set of 10 reps with the right leg and then 10 reps with the left.

- Rest 30 seconds.

- Do another 10 reps on each side.

- Rest 30 seconds.

- Do the last set of 10 on each side.

- Then rest a minute or two before commencing with the next technique, shin kick to the groin.

MAKING IT AN AEROBIC EXERCISE

When you feel you can increase the intensity—usually after a month of consistent training—don't rest at all between sets. So if you were, say, practicing elbow strikes, you would do 10 with each arm without stopping, and continue until you have completed all three sets. Then you can rest for 2 minutes before starting to practice the next technique.

When you feel you can increase the intensity again—say, after four to eight weeks of not resting between sets—don't rest at all between the seven techniques: you go through all the sets and reps of all seven techniques without stopping. This way you're not only working to improve the quality of your techniques but you're working aerobically, too. You're improving your skill, your health, and you're burning off that Cinnabon.

When you execute the techniques at medium to fast speed, it will take about 8 minutes to complete all the sets and reps nonstop. While this might have you huffing and puffing, you need to go for 20 minutes to get the minimum aerobic benefit. So simply take a 1- or 2-minute break after doing all the nonstop sets and reps and then go through them again. If it takes you 8 minutes each time, you now have 16 minutes invested in your workout. Choose one or two techniques that need extra work and do them again for 4 or 5 minutes to give you a good 20-minute workout.

Stick with that for two to three weeks and then go through all seven techniques three times to give you 24 minutes of strength building, speed building, coordination building, muscle and brain ingraining, and ugly calorie burning. Compare all these benefits against climbing a Stairmaster to nowhere.

It's critical that you don't sacrifice the quality of your techniques to have a good cardio workout. More on that in a moment.

SPEED

Practicing your techniques fast before you're ready promotes sloppy and ineffective moves. Initial learning and ingraining is most effective when you move slowly to ensure the quality of your movements as well as your understanding of them. Once you feel comfortable that your technique is of good quality, then, and only then, should you begin to increase your speed. Also know that there will be workouts in which you feel clumsy and out of sorts. Don't worry about it as that happens from time to time. When it does, simply slow down and enjoy an easy workout that emphasizes good form. If you feel better next time, speed things up.

Just because you can go fast with one technique does not mean you're ready to go fast with another. If you find that you're performing sloppily with a particular move, although you can do the others with good form, speed and power, keep working slowly on the sloppy one until it's no longer a problem. Once you're sure it's okay, slowly increase the speed over the next two or three workouts.

There is no hurry to go fast (sort of a pun). Develop proper delivery first and then push the speed.

"When you want to know more" techniques

You're ready to add the slaps, forearm strikes, stomps and knee strikes from Chapter Four "When you want to know more" to your workout. Simply follow the same format as just described for "The least you need to know" techniques.

- Slaps: 3 sets, 10 reps, each side
- Forearm strikes: 3 sets, 10 reps, each side
- Stomps: 3 sets, 10 reps, each side
- Knees: 3 sets, 10 reps, each side

AEROBICALLY

Since there are only four techniques, as compared to seven in the last workout, you will have to repeat all four techniques three or four times to get in the minimum 20 minutes. Do 3 sets of 10 reps on each side of each technique and, as you did with "The least you need to know" movements, don't rest after each set but do rest 2 minutes between techniques. After three or four weeks, don't rest at all—do all the sets and reps nonstop—until you have trained for at least 20 minutes.

THESE ARE NOT DANCE MOVES

Don't get so involved in the aerobic part of your training that the quality of your technique suffers. Your first objective is to develop effective self-defense moves and then your aerobic fitness. You don't want to turn your training session into a kicking and punching dance workout that you see advertised on late-night infomercials. Yes, these DVDs do provide good exercise but they don't teach self-defense because they are not executed with sufficient speed, power and intent, all absolute requirements to stop an attacker who wants to hurt, rape or kill you. They are dance moves. Period.

Although at first hesitant, we decided to include aerobic routines because when done correctly they develop your self-defense skills as they improve your fitness level. "Correctly" means that you execute each repetition with the intent to stop an attacker. Even when practicing at slow to medium speed, your mental intent should be present in each move.

If you find yourself performing your moves as if they were a dance routine, cease training aerobically as you will do more harm than good.

Combining the Workouts

Let's say that three or four months have passed and you feel good about your progress with the techniques in both chapters. Now you want to kick up your training even more by combining the techniques from both into one workout. This makes for a good training session, albeit a hard one. Here is how to do it:

- Combine the 11 techniques from both chapters and reduce the volume you're doing to 2 sets of 10 reps of each move.

- After three or four weeks, increase to 3 sets of 10 reps of each technique.

- After three or four weeks, increase the number of sets or the number of reps, or both. If you're happy remaining at 3 sets of 10 reps, that is okay.

- Take rest breaks whenever you want.

- To train aerobically, follow the suggestions described above to reduce your rest periods. Train for a minimum of 20 minutes.

After you have added all of the techniques, it looks like this.

- Hammerfist: 3 sets, 10 reps, each side

- Claws: 3 sets, 10 reps, each side

- Palm-heel strikes: 3 sets, 10 reps each side

- Elbows: 3 sets, 10 reps, each side

- Front kick: 3 sets, 10 reps, each side

- Side stomp kick: 3 sets, 10 reps each side

- Shin kick: 3 sets, 10 reps, each side

- Slaps: 3 sets, 10 reps, each side

- Stomps: 3 sets, 10 reps, each side

- Forearm strikes: 3 sets, 10 reps, each side

- Knees: 3 sets, 10 reps, each

Combining Exercises With Self-defense

There are two ways you can incorporate the body weight exercises we covered in Chapter Seven, "Getting strong now."

TRAIN THEM ON SEPARATE DAYS

You can do the bodyweight exercises two times a week on, say, Tuesday and Thursday and then practice your self-defense techniques on Monday, Wednesday and Friday. That approach looks like this:

- Monday: Self-defense techniques

- Tuesday: Bodyweight exercises

- Wednesday: Self-defense techniques

- Thursday: Bodyweight exercises

- Friday: Self-defense exercises

Or you can eliminate the self-defense practice on Friday. Now it looks like this:

- Monday: Self-defense techniques

- Tuesday: Bodyweight exercises

- Wednesday: Self-defense techniques

- Thursday: Bodyweight exercises

This gives you a solid week of training with your weekends free to relax and hit the banana splits. Kidding. Kidding!

BODYWEIGHT EXERCISES AND SELF-DEFENSE ON THE SAME DAY

If you prefer to train just two times a week, you can combine the body weight training with self-defense training, say, on Monday and Thursday. It's important to have two rest days in between. If you're out of shape, we suggest that you wait a few months until you're in better condition before you try this approach.

Monday: Bodyweight exercise followed by self-defense techniques

Thursday: Bodyweight exercise followed by self-defense techniques

Nonaerobic: If you want to combine everything and you're physically ready, do your pushups, core training and squats first, followed by your self-defense techniques. Rest whenever you want.

Aerobic: This is tough so you need to be in good shape before you attempt it. To train everything aerobically, we suggest you begin by doing pushups, core exercises and squats first, 4 sets of each, then rest for a couple of minutes. Then commence doing the 11 self-defense moves. Here is how it looks with rest breaks.

- 1 set of pushups, followed without rest by…

- 1 set of core exercise, followed without rest by…

- 1 set of squats.

- Rest 20 seconds, and repeat the three exercises again.

- Rest 20 seconds, and repeat the three exercises again.

- Rest 20 seconds, and repeat the three exercises again.

- Rest 1 or 2 minutes and then commence with the self-defense techniques nonstop until you have completed 3 sets of 10 reps of all the moves you want to do. You can either do the techniques from "The least you need to know" or "When you want to know more," or if you really want to kick it, combine all of them.

Practice in a variety of settings

Too often in self-defense training and even in on-going martial arts schools, students get locked into using techniques only one way. For example, too many spend years practicing punching straight forward from their fighting stance. While their blows eventually become fast and powerful, many don't consider training their punch against an imaginary opponent who is standing above them on a set of stairs, lying below them on the ground, or sitting beside them in a car. Ironically, it's in these other positions that they will likely have to use that punch. Fortunately, it's an easy fix.

Consider the palm-heel strike.

Assume your stance with your left foot forward and pop out 10 right-hand palm-heel strikes. Now switch your stance to right foot forward and do 10 reps with your left hand. Repeat 2 times, totaling 20 reps with each arm.

You're not done yet; you still have 80 more reps to do with each arm. Did we forget to mention that you're going to do 100 reps? Whoops, sorry. Will you be tired after? Yes. Will you have a better grasp of this strike than if you were to do all 100 reps the same way as just described? Definitely.

Let's do the rest of your palm-heel session.

SIT IN A CHAIR

Begin by holding your palms up in front of you as if you were warding off someone. Because you're sitting, you can't rotate your hips when you hit. Therefore, you must draw your power from the rotation of your waist and the sudden and hard tensing of your stomach muscles at the end of your strike. Do 2 sets of 10 reps with each arm concentrating on getting as much power out of the blows without the benefit of your hips.

LIE ON YOUR BACK

Hold your palms up as of warding off someone who is leaning down to grab you or someone trying to climb on top of you. Then strike upward with your right palm-heel. Be careful retracting your other arm because you can bang your elbow into the floor. Pay attention to how your blows feel. Can you get more power when you tense your chest and stomach at the end of the blow? Yes. Can you get more power and greater reach if you twist to the side a little? Yes. Do 2 sets of 10 reps with each arm.

SIT BEHIND THE WHEEL OF YOUR CAR

Shoot out 10 palm-heel strikes toward the passenger side as if hitting an attacker who has climbed in. Then open your driver's door and fire 10 reps of your left palm-heel with your left hand as if striking someone trying to pull you out of the seat. Observe what helps to harness power from this somewhat cramped position. Does it help to rotate your upper body a little away from the blow? (Example: rotate a little to your right when thrusting with your left palm.) Yes it does. What else helps? What are your limitations? Do 2 sets of 10 reps with each arm.

STANDING ON STAIRS

Get into the best punching position you can with one foot a step or two higher than the other one. Launch a rear hand palm-heel strike at an imaginary person standing below you. How is your balance? Awkward, eh? Be careful you don't launch yourself down the stairs. Now do 9 more reps. Switch feet and punch with your other arm. What adjustments do you have to make on the uneven terrain?

For the second set of 10 reps, strike upward at an imaginary attacker. Are you more stable if you bend your legs more? Yes. If it makes your legs shaky, check out the squat exercise in Chapter Seven, "Getting strong now." Do 2 sets of 10 reps of palm-heel strikes on each side. Do 20 reps punching up the stairs and 20 punching down.

You're done. That is 100 palm-heel strikes with each hand in five different positions. How do you feel? You might be tired but you now possess far more knowledge about the palm-heel strike than you did when just punching straight ahead. Also, your mind is now open to using the technique in positions other than standing upright and punching forward.

We strongly encourage you to practice all of your techniques in as many places as you can imagine. No place is too weird for the simple reason that you can be attacked anywhere. Here are just a few.

KICKS AND KNEE STRIKES

- Practice on a floor cluttered with toys, newspapers, clothes, etc.

- Practice on stairs.

- Practice while wearing tight pants or a skirt.

- Practice with your back to a wall.

- Practice in a variety of shoes

HAND, FOREARM AND ELBOW TECHNIQUES

- Practice while wearing a restrictive top.

- Practice with your back to a wall.

- Practice in a corner.

- Practice in a small space: bathroom, closet, corner of your basement.

- Practice on your knees.

It's not how many techniques you know but how well you understand the few you do. Understanding comes from practicing them in a large variety of ways.

Hitting things

If you don't have anyone to hold a pad, shield or heavy bag, you're going to have to get innovative. Fortunately, it's not that hard. The pieces of equipment Lisa is demonstrating on here cost under $100. Less when you can get them used.

Hitting things is fun and beneficial. Striking a hand-held pad and a small heavy bag allows you to feel what it's like to hit a human. You also discover small ways to adjust your hand and foot for optimum hitting power, and to reduce injury.

You don't have to hit the pad and bag as hard as you can every time you train. In fact, it can be painful to your joints to strike the hand-held pad hard when it's on the floor or attached to a post. This is because the pad doesn't move with your blows as it does when someone holds it for you. Nonetheless, you can hit at half power and still benefit.

The heavy bag is thick enough that you can palm-heel it and kick it full power, and not have to worry about your joints. To reiterate, you don't half to hit full power every workout.

PRACTICE HITTING A HAND-HELD PAD ON THE FLOOR

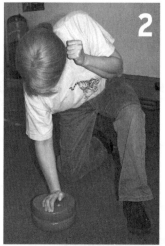

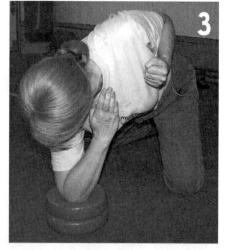

Hit it with your hammerfist as if striking a downed attacker's nose (1). Palm-heel it as if striking a downed attacker's face (2) . Elbow it as if hitting a downed attacker's neck (3).

Stomp it as if kicking a downed attacker's hand or knee (4-5).

PRACTICE HITTING A HAND-HELD PAD ATTACHED TO A POST

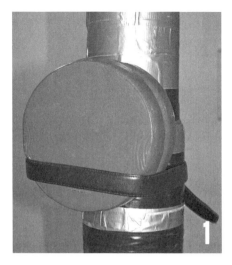

Secure a hand-held pad to a post with a pants belt.

Palm-heel it as if hitting an attacker's nose.

Elbow it as if hitting an attacker's chin.

Hammerfist it as if hitting an attacker's throat (4). Claw as if shredding an attacker's face (5).

ATTACH A HEAVY BAG TO A POST

Front kick it as if kicking an attacker's knee or thigh.

Side stomp it as if kicking an attacker's thigh, knee or shin.

Palm-heel it as if striking a downed attacker.

CLAWING PAPER

Practice clawing through newspaper...

...as if clawing down an attacker's face. Can you claw through a Sunday paper?

TRAINING WITH A PARTNER

So many women have told us that their husbands and boyfriends were awful as a training partner. They criticized the women's efforts and went out of their way to make them feel foolish and incompetent. If you have one of these and he continues to undermine your training after you ask him not to, find someone else to work with you. Your training partners should help you improve and you should help them improve.

Holding the hand-held pads and bag for each other is an important responsibility. The holder's job is to point out errors, give you a variety of heights and angles, move about slowly so you can practice your footwork, and ensure that the bag is held solidly so that you don't sprain a wrist or ankle.

The subject of how to train with a partner has filled volumes; Loren and others have written on the subject extensively. We list a few of his books and DVDs in "Resources" at the end of this book.

HITTING HANDS

Practice hitting your partner's hands to work combinations. He can move them closer or farther apart, or hold one high and the other low. Your job is to hit them with whatever technique you want, one right after the other. Don't hit them hard since they're stuffed with bones, cartilage and nerve endings.

You can simulate that the attacker is moving. First, hit him with one palm-heel strike...

...and when he moves a little to one side, hit him with your other.

KICKING SHIELD

A kicking shield is a light-weight pad of varying thickness. Your partner can move it all around so that you have to use footwork to hit it at the best angle. Your bag person can also tie it to her torso and then stalk you so that you get a sense of hitting someone who is moving toward you aggressively (1). Front kick it as if kicking an attacker's bladder (2). Side stomp it as if kicking an attacker in the upper thigh or bladder (3).

Kick it as if hitting an attacker's shin.

Hand-held pads come in all sizes and shapes.

You can palm-heel it, claw it, and hammerfist it. Or you can kick it with your lower shin (as pictured) as if hitting an attacker's groin.

DUMMY HEAD

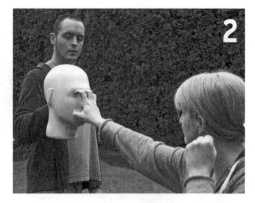

This is a nifty striking pad with facial features (1). Claw it as if shredding an attacker's face (2).

Self-defense is a serious subject but that doesn't mean your practice can't be fun. The more enjoyable it is, the more you will look forward to doing it. You will like seeing and feeling your techniques improve. You will like how your body feels and looks, and how your sense of confidence gives you a positive outlook on all aspects of your life.

Here are some quotes about practice that we like:

"The more I practice, the luckier I get." - Jerry Barber, about golf

"Practice puts your brains in your muscles." - Sam Snead, about golf

"Practice is the best master." – Author unknown

"You can't hire someone to practice for you."- Author unknown

"The more you sweat in practice, the less you bleed in battle."- Author Unknown

mind power

"IT IS ESSENTIAL TO SEE BOTH SIDES WITHOUT MOVING THE
EYEBALLS." ~ MIYAMOTO MUSASHI, SAMURAI

How do you teach alertness and assessing a situation?

We possibly have more natural intuition than men do that allows us to detect danger earlier and therefore avoid a confrontation altogether. Also, because we are less apt to rely on our muscular strength, we can be better at getting out of the way instead of pushing back. I don't get hot headed, as I see guys often get, where they feel a need to defend their masculinity in some way. I can't think of something someone would say to me that would make me feel I needed to defend my ego.

■ ■ ■

I think some women have to learn that they do have power and can control what happens to them. They have to understand the force they can exhibit and not act like a victim.

■ ■ ■

Recently, a man was walking towards me at a traffic light. As I approached the light, it turned red and I had to wait. He should have kept walking in the other direction and didn't. I went on alert at that moment. He asked me for the time. I told him. He asked if he could say something to me. I said no. He repeated this and then put his hand on my shoulder. I flung his hand off and told him that if he touched me again, I would break his arm. I may have over-reacted, but he did leave and ultimately, no harm done.

■ ■ ■

I teach situational awareness, so that when a woman sees something that just doesn't look right, they must be on alert. If that person's movements correlate with theirs, then they must be at a higher alert level.

CHAPTER NINE

ASSESSING A THREAT

Let's examine certain characteristics that are common among attackers, whether it's a spouse, partner, friend, relative, work associate or stranger. It's sad to think that so many people—even friends and relatives—could be a threat to your safety, but that is the simple, harsh reality backed by bloody statistics that number in the hundreds of thousands each year.

As always, awareness of what is going on around you is your first line of defense. Yes, we have said this before and we will say it again because it's a critical aspect of being safe. So is knowing how to assess what is going on.

Ignoring a Threat Won't Make it Go Away

Riding the commuter train after dark in our town is often dangerous. On one occasion, about a dozen gangbangers ran onto the train, all dressed the same in baggy, brown khaki pants, white t-shirts, hairnets, and arms tattooed to denote their gang affiliation. They shouted, cursed loudly and flashed gang signs as they sauntered up and down the aisle. A few regular commuters kept an eye on them but the majority ignored the dangerous reality and buried their heads in their fictional novels. One woman sat knitting, as if moving the threads about would hide the danger that was within arm's reach of her. At least she was armed! That is, if she were to think of those needles as weapons.

"Be Alert. Be Aware"

The following list of characteristics pertains to both strangers and people you know. They might not mean anything as far as your safety is concerned or they could mean everything. Since you don't know, you must continue your awareness and assessment as long as that person is within your sight.

Throughout this chapter, we tell you to "think weapons." This applies to your personal body weapons—claws, palm-heels, forearms, knees and feet—as well as any object within your reach that you can use for your defense and offense.

Is He Angry?

Here are a few signs that the person standing before you is in a rage. Not every angry person strikes out, but since you might not know the one in your face, it's important to be aware of his every move—and get away from him as soon as you're able.

HE IS SHAKING

If it's not cold out and he is shaking like a fall leaf, you got to wonder why. People who are high on drugs shake and so do angry people. He might be shaking because he is filled with adrenaline over what he is about to do to you.

Avoid this person. If you can't, and he has confronted you, position yourself so there is something between the two of you: chair, parking meter, car fender or table. Think weapons: What do you have in your purse? What is within reach?

HE IS HOLDING HIS SHOULDERS HIGH

An angry person typically lifts his shoulders (Photo 1). You do it when you're mad, and so does the road rager and your partner. If it's a stranger confronting you, back away, get something between you and think weapons. If it's someone you know and they have a history of acting out physically when angry, leave, or if you can't, get something between you and think weapons.

HE IS CLENCHING HIS HANDS

Enraged people often clench and open one or both hands repeatedly as a pre-assault indicator (Photo 2). It might be a nervous twitch or it could be because their mind is ahead of their action. Consider this a godsend because it gives you an extra moment to get away, create distance, get behind something, and obtain a weapon.

HIS IS TENSING HIS NECK

When someone is angry, really angry, they tense their neck, a result of clenching their jaw (Photo 3). Is tightening his neck muscles all that he is going to do? Or is he going to ignite? You don't know. Therefore, it's important that you create distance from this person, assume the "leave-me-alone" stance with your hands up and palms toward the threat. As noted earlier, this sometimes has a calming effect on upset people—but not

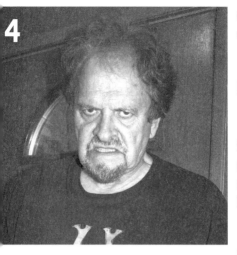

everyone. Get something between you and the threat and watch him carefully. If you can get away, do so.

HE IS CLENCHING HIS TEETH

This is closely related to a taught neck, since it's virtually impossible to clamp down on your teeth without tensing those muscles (Photo 4). When someone confronts you in a such a fashion, they just might be on the verge of violence. Create distance, speak calmly, and know what potential weapons are within reach.

HE IS CURSING

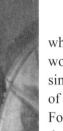

In today's culture, some people curse like sailors and don't care who is within earshot. When someone says that their !*#!*& car wouldn't start or their !@#$ boss is giving them a hard time they are simply (and crudely) expressing themselves. But when cursing is part of other characteristics we are discussing here, it should not be ignored. For example, when someone is standing in front of you clenching their fists, holding their shoulders high, tightening their neck muscles, and cursing at you through clenched teeth, that is a person barely constraining their rage. Create space between you and the threat, get away if you can, and think weapons.

HE IS DOING THE GERMAN SHEPHERD STARE

When a German shepherd is thinking seriously about attacking you, he often stares off to the side, as if another zone, and emits a low, guttural rumble. Loren worked with German shepherds in the Army and witnessed this pre-attack many times. Later, when working as a police officer, he saw people who were on the verge of going berserk demonstrate this same stare (Photo 5). In his experience, your gift for gab and knowledge of psychology 101 will not work because the individual's mind is in a place that isn't receptive. If you can't escape, grab something to use as a weapon, and try to get something between the two of you to slow his attack.

Pop quiz: Right now, close your eyes and say aloud all the potential weapons within your reach. How did you do? Give yourself this quiz once or twice a day.

What is He Saying?

When the police respond to an assault call, they always ask what the attacker said before, during and after the incident. Words are important; don't ignore them. Unfortunately, some people don't get this. "He threatened me," victims often say, "but I didn't think he really meant it." Clearly, their opinion was wrong.

When someone—spouse, partner, friend, or stranger—says they are going to _____ (fill in the blank) to you, believe it. Police departments, the military and the CIA would pay a load of money for this kind of advanced intelligence information. One more time: When a threat tells you that he is going to—punch you, kick you, choke you, steal your car, steal your money, or hurt your child—believe it and respond accordingly.

IS HE HIGH?

Drug intoxication makes a volatile person even more dangerous. It's hard to talk to someone flying high because his brain is under the influence. He might see the world as being in a deep fog and populated with monsters. Or it might be one in which everything is distorted and confused. If he is experiencing these things and he is angry at you, or you're simply in the wrong place at the wrong time, he might feel compelled to strike out.

HE IS BREATHING HARD

A person high on drugs might be breathing hard, as if he had just run up a flight of steps. When combined with other characteristics noted here, it's almost a sure sign of a drug high. Create distance from him, get something between the two of you, and think weapons.

HE IS CURSING

As mentioned in the last section, cursing by itself might not mean much but when it's uttered in one, long steady stream, or spoken as rapidly as a firing machine gun, it can be a sign that the speaker is under the influence of drugs and on the edge of violence.

Feeling no pain and super strength

When Loren was a cop, he or his partners witnessed people who were high on drugs exhibit extreme tolerance to pain and extraordinary strength. For example, they saw people:

- fry their hands in a hot skillet.
- pull their teeth out with pliers.
- break handcuffs.
- break heavy leather hospital gurney restraints.
- not react to being shot.
- not react to being stabbed.
- not react to the pain of self-circumcision with a hunting knife.

Drug-sopped people with such great strength and invulnerability to pain will eat your groin kicks and palm-heel strikes like M&Ms, which is why we emphasize the importance of getting away from them.

HE IS TALKING TOO SLOWLY OR TOO FAST

If. He. Talks. Like. This. or ifhetalkslikethis, and shows other drug-related symptoms, give him some space, a lot of it. Both slow and fast speech is dangerous. Don't be fooled into thinking that a slow speech pattern means he is a mellow person. Slow talkers can erupt into violence just as quickly as fast ones. Get something between the two of you and get away from him as soon as you're able.

HE IS MOVING TOO SLOWLY OR TOO FAST

This is the same as "talking too slowly or talking too fast." Don't be fooled into thinking that someone moving as if caught in a vat of heavy glue is less dangerous than the quick, jerky types. Both are unpredictable. Get away from them, get something between you, and think weapons.

HE IS BABBLING

This is a classic sign of drug intoxication. When the individual says something that sounds like this, "F*ghj!rd7opids^jd!" he isn't about to listen to your well-meaning words. Get away, get something between you, and think weapons.

HE IS SCREAMING

This is a common reaction to a violent drug high and can be especially frightening when the person is doing it in your face. While screaming isn't justification to groin kick the loud mouth, it's certainly a good reason to get away, get something between you and think about what you can use for a weapon.

HE HAS A FLUSHED FACE AND HE IS SWEATING

By itself, sweating might be an indication of the swine flu, but when it's in conjunction with other characteristics listed here, it's a good sign that the person is high. Don't dab him with a tissue but get away from him, get something between you, and think about what you can use for a weapon.

Visual Cues of a Good Fighter or a Dangerous Person

You can't tell by looking. Never is that expression more meaningful than when talking about someone's ability to reap physical violence. Case in point: An office copy machine repairman was working on a machine near Loren's desk when he noticed a photo of Loren and his 10-year-old daughter, both wearing martial arts uniforms. He asked Loren if he trained and Loren told him that he was an instructor. This seemed to delight the repairman who looked to be in his mid 20s, skinny as a pencil, with a protruding Adam's apple, bad complexion, a piece of tape holding his glasses together and a cluster of pens and pencils jammed into his shirt pocket.

"I train, too," the young man said.

Loren nodded, chewing on the inside of cheeks so as not to smile. "Maybe you would like to come to a seminar I'm hosting this Saturday," Loren said. "We're bringing up a high-ranking jujitsu instructor from San Francisco." To his surprise, the man quickly accepted the invitation.

Loren was doubly surprised on Saturday when the geeky-looking man showed up wearing a black belt and quickly established that he was one of the best fighters out of all of the attendees. He executed his techniques flawlessly and with extraordinary speed and power.

On the flip side, one of Loren's partners had to arrest the current Mr. Universe at the time, a man who was as big as a dump truck and who had graced the cover of every bodybuilding magazine. Not only did the man break down and cry like a one-year-old, he ran into the bathroom, locked the door and refused to come out until the smaller-than-average officer promised not to hurt him.

For sure, *you can't always tell by looking.* Therefore, consider the information in this subsection as only a rough guide.

HE HAS AN ATHLETIC BUILD

This person is likely in good physical shape and has the confidence of someone who knows his body, its strength, speed, endurance and skills. Even if he has never trained in a fighting art and his fitness is a result of shooting baskets with the guys three times a week, his confidence makes him a threat.

HE IS A SMALL MAN WITH A LIGHT, BALANCED STRIDE

This characteristic often indicates a degree of fitness and body awareness. You should also expect quick limb speed and fast, evasive body movements.

HE IS A BIG MAN WITH AN EASY, SWINGING STRIDE

Have you ever seen an especially big man who dances gracefully? There are not many but they are out there, and it's a marvel to watch. A big man with a comfortable, relaxed gate is a person who is body aware, and confident in himself and his abilities.

HE DOES NOT STRUT OR POSTURE

Loren is friends with several SWAT members, officers who train constantly in all facets of fighting. After all, it's SWAT that other cops call. While these officers are highly trained in hand-to-hand, a variety of firearms, explosives, and advanced tactics, nearly all are quiet and humble. You would never guess by looking at them that they could easily level an entire community.

Be careful of the quiet one, the one who has no need to threaten or to boast. He just might be the most dangerous of all.

The above characteristics are common among those people who are physically fit, confident and possess knowledge as to how to cause injury and pain. Of course, not all people who possess these things are violent or abusive. But when they are coupled with threats, a history of physical assault, intoxication, and rage, they can be a dangerous mix.

To reiterate, whether you're dealing with an abusive partner, drunk friend at a party, an acquaintance in a club, or a stranger on the street, keep in mind that you can't always tell by looking. Be in the Yellow Zone.

Reading his intentions

Sometimes it's easy to determine the attacker's intentions. For example:

HE TELLS YOU

This erases all doubt. When your spouse says he is going to punish you for not having his dinner ready, and he has a history of hitting you after telling you this, you know exactly what he is going to do. If a man in a nightclub accuses you of leading him on, and says, "If you're not going to give it to me then I'm going to take it," you have an idea of what he is going to do. If you tell a boyfriend that you don't want to see him again, and he says he is going to cut up your face so no other guy will want you, you know what he is going to do.

Don't convince yourself that people don't mean what they say. With these kinds of veiled and not so veiled threats, especially if there has been physical violence in the past, you know what he means and you should do what is necessary to prevent it from happening again. Escape is your first option, attacking him is your second.

Preemptive hitting can get dicey in court as well as with the responding police officers, especially if you don't have physical marks that show that he assaulted you. However, if you're absolutely convinced you're about to be physically attacked, you can articulate why you believe this, and there is a history of it, in most jurisdictions you can defend yourself preemptively. Check with the laws where you live to be sure. Call your local police agency or call the district attorney.

Think about this now. What would someone have to say to you to justify attacking him first? Factor in such elements as how close he is to you, his word choice, the way he gestures, and what his friends are saying and doing. Don't wait until you're in the middle of the event to decide what to do.

HIS ACTIONS

Be alert as what he is saying and doing.

- He is removing his belt as he says, "You're going to get a beating."

- He has thrown an object at you in the past, such as a coffee cup, book, glass, beer bottle. He is picking up one now and threatening to hit you with it.

- He is moving toward a place where you know there are weapons, such as a drawer, cabinet, or glove box.

Too many victims say that they didn't think the guy would hurt them, although the attacker told them that that was what he was going to do. Don't fall victim to believing that all people are good, that violence only happens to others, and that so-and-so would never hurt you. Believe it and take actions to prevent it and defend against it.

Does the threat have a weapon?

Here are some things the police watch for when dealing with people. Should you see these indicators, immediately get away from the person. Never worry that you might be overreacting or that you might offend him. If your gut tells you that this person is dangerous, get away from him.

- He is wearing a heavy coat when it's warm outside.

  - This can be a way to conceal a weapon. Gang members wear big coats as a fashion statement as well as to conceal weapons.

- He is wearing a knife sheath.

  - Some street people or transient types often carry knives in a sheath.

- He touches his side frequently.

    o People who are not used to carrying a weapon under their jackets will touch their side often to ensure that it's still there.

- He holds his arm out to the side.

    o People who are not used to carrying a weapon under their jackets will hold their arms out to their side.

- He holds his arm behind his back.

    o Most often, people carry weapons in the small of the back. An armed person will suddenly reach behind him or he will continually hold one hand behind him as he talks.

- He folds his arms across his chest.

    o Some street fighters use this as an on-guard stance or to conceal a weapon in their hand.

- He reaches into his backpack.

    o This is a common place to carry a weapon.

If someone displaying one of these characteristic confronts you, be on guard for a weapon, get a car fender or trashcan between you, and get away as soon as you can.

What range is he in?

Let's say the situation has deteriorated to the extent that violence is inevitable, such as:

- You recognize all the indicators that your husband is about to assault you.

- A verbally abusive boyfriend is about to get physical.

- An over-the-top angry co-worker is near you when he begins to act out violently.

- An aggressive drunk man becomes enraged when you decline to dance with him.

- An aggressive street panhandler will not let you pass until you give him money.

- A man steps out of the shadows between your garage and your house, his eyes glassed over, his fists clenched and he is angrily muttering something.

These situations are seconds away from violence. You know this because your alertness and awareness are on the job; you know this because you have perceived the cues just discussed; and you know this because you're not in denial.

RANGE

Let's look at the distance between you and the threat. Martial artist call this space "range" and police officers call it "the gap." Martial artists monitor the range to see how their opponent might cross it to attack. They also monitor it to determine the best way to cross it to kick, punch, or grapple their opponents. Cops watch the gap to see that the suspect does not get too close and to determine the safest way to cross it to take the person into custody. Crossing the range skillfully often determines the winner of a martial arts match while crossing it tactically can be a matter of life and death for a cop.

KICKING RANGE

Kicking range is one that is greater than your arm's reach (though you can stomp, and shin kick much closer). It's true for the potential attacker and it's true for your kicks.

Some skilled martial artists can stand virtually chest to chest with you and still kick you in the head. Fortunately, these people are rare. Untrained people need distance. You need it to land your front kick and side stomp kick, and so does the attacker.

How do you know when he is going to kick? That can be a tough call. It's an easy one if he says he is going to kick you—"I'm gonna kick your head in!"—or he has shown that he is a kicker: He just kicked a lamp, your car door, a pet, or he has kicked you in the past. When Loren got a police call about a man kicking out store windows or kicking another person, he would watch the man's feet and maintain a large gap until it was time to move in and take him down.

When you think the threat is a kicker:

When the threat starts to kick...

- Maintain a range that is greater than his leg reach. This forces him to take a step before he can kick, which gives you an extra second or two to react.

- When the attacker steps toward you, step back to maintain the range.

- Get something between the two of you: chair, trashcan, car fender, or tree.

- Move around while staying outside his range. Untrained kickers need you to be still.

- When he starts to kick, throw something at him to distract the process (right).

- One of the best ways to disrupt his mindset to kick you, and one that poses great risk, is to cross that range quickly and attack him first (as illustrated in the sequence on the next page).

...throw something into his face to disrupt him physically and mentally. Then flee or attack him.

Lunge forward with your lead leg and slam a lead-hand palm-heel strike into his chin.

Look for the moment to attack the kicker. If he is drunk, he might stumble before kicking. If he is sober, look for a moment when he is distracted ever so briefly.

Without hesitation, hit him with a right palm-heel strike.

Then another left (4). Then another right (5). You might have to shuffle forward a little if the first blows knocked him back a step or two. Don't' think of this combination as: hit and then hit and then hit. Think: hithithithit.

The side of the jaw, from the front all the way back to where it angles up toward the ear, is a highly effective target that jars the head and the brain. It's a potential knock out point, too.

WHEN YOU WANT TO KICK:

As we've discussed earlier, a kick can generate tremendous force and injury, but it carries with it some inherent risks, even for veteran martial artists. Consider the following points.

Concerns:

- Anytime one leg leaves the ground, only one leg supports the body.

- Kicking, depending on the floor or ground surface—wet grass, wet pavement slick tile, loose rug—can cause your support foot to slip out from under you.

- The attacker can capture a kick that is too high or too slow.

- An untrained kick might injure your foot or ankle.

You should:

- train hard so that you're confident in your kicks.

- only kick when you're on a non-slick surface.

- know that you have the skill to cross that space quickly to deliver your kick.

- kick to vulnerable areas: shin, groin, face, hands, fingers, and ankle.

- kick multiple times when the situation allows.

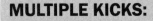

MULTIPLE KICKS:

From the leave-me-alone stance, lunge forward to close the space...

...and ram the ball of your foot into his shin.

When he reacts in pain, kick him in the groin.

HAND AND ARM RANGE

Since the hand and arm range is right on the edge of your discomfort zone, this is a good place to talk about an important fighting principle.

ACTION/REACTION PRINCIPLE:

Loren taught the action/reaction principle to police officers for years, many of whom said later that it saved them from serious injury.

A principle is a law that doesn't change. For example, the principle of gravity is in play when you throw an apple into the air and it comes back down. There are different ways you can launch it into the air, such as overhand and underhand, which is the application of technique to the principle. In the end, though, gravity is the constant.

The principle of action/reaction states that action is faster than reaction. For our purposes, let's say that a threat is within arm's reach of you. Should he decide to smack you upside the head, he will likely have success because his close proximity makes it difficult for you to react in time. Here is why.

To hit you, he first has to decide to do so. The idea bounces around in his brain before a message shoots down to his arm and shoulder muscles to cock his hand, swing his arm outward, and make contact with the side of your face with his palm.

Because the decision to do it and how to do it took place in his brain, you have no clue that he is thinking about hitting you until you see his hand rushing toward your face. Your eyes have to see the hand, your eyes must send the image of the threat to your brain, where it bounces around from post to post until the last one lights up and flashes: "A hand speeding toward my face is not a good thing!" Then the brain sends a message down to your body to block it, duck it, or in some way prevent it from hitting you.

Should he start to fall, chamber your leg...

...and stomp his fingers. Then run.

Crushing the nerves in the hands is debilitating and so painful that all of his attention will focus on them, giving you a moment to hit him again or flee.

Here is the problem. Because you're standing so close, there is not enough time for you to block or avoid it. So you're hit.

The way to increase your odds is to stand a little farther than arm's reach from the threat. He might still decide to hit you but to actually do so, he has to step or jump across the range between you to make contact. This gives you a second or so longer to react. It's not much, but it's enough for you to block or evade his blow.

War story: A police officer who had recently been in one of Loren's in-service training classes contacted him to say thanks for emphasizing the action/reaction principle. He told Loren that he had stopped a street person one night to ask him a question. As taught, the officer maintained a distance a little greater than arm's reach from the man.

At one point, the man pulled a pencil from his pocket as if to write something down. When he abruptly cocked back his arm, the officer saw a flash of streetlight reflect off the end of it. The cop sidestepped the blow, dumped the man to the sidewalk and handcuffed him. Upon examining the pencil, the officer found the reason for the light reflection. Imbedded in the eraser was a doubled-sided razor blade.

In hand and arm range, you're close enough to hit the attacker with your hand, forearm or elbow. As mentioned earlier, always remember that if you can hit him, he can hit you. We emphasize this because so many people don't factor this in. Never get so focused on what you're going to do that you can't see what he can do.

Put your hands up in the leave-me-alone stance and strive to control the space between you and the threat. Say loudly, "Leave me alone! Don't come any closer!" to warn him and to draw the attention of others.

"Leave me alone!"

Shout these three words whenever you feel a threat from someone, whether you're in the middle of the grocery, on a public sidewalk, in a bar, or in your own home. They are powerful words that are virtually impossible to misunderstand; they might even have a jarring effect on a violent partner.

Say it with enough volume that people outside your house can hear it, especially when doors or windows are open. Third party complaintants often call the police on a domestic violence situation because they heard these words or similar ones coming from the house in question. Anecdotal evidence shows that when someone shouts "leave me alone!" out in public, it attracts people. It lets others know what is going on. Additionally, when others hear it they become witnesses.

WATCH HIS HANDS:

One of the first things cops learn in the academy is to watch the hands. Hands can hurt and hands can kill, it's as simple as that. How many times have you heard the police in the movies tell people to "Keep your hands where I can see them"? For sure, a quick movement by the suspect—he reaches behind his back, he plunges his hand into a pants pocket, he moves to retrieve something from a backpack—can result in the suspect kissing the sidewalk, or worse. *Hands can hurt and hands can kill. Watch them.*

- Your angry and volatile partner is screaming at you—watch his hands.

- The angry motorist stomps toward you as you get out of your car—watch his hands.

- The obnoxious drunk in the bar is angry because you just shot him down—watch his hands.

- The cranky panhandler is blocking your path—watch his hands.

The instant your alertness and awareness tells you that this person is dangerous, focus on his hands. It takes him only a second to pick up a bottle, chair, hammer, or a thousand other things in the heat of his rage, intoxication, or mental illness. One moment it's a framed photo of you and your spouse on vacation and within an instant it's a weapon to bludgeon you. One second earlier, there wasn't even a remote thought in your mind that he could use that beautiful frozen moment that the two of you once shared as a weapon against you. There probably was not one in his mind, either. Such can be the intensity and explosiveness of domestic violence. That is why you must watch the hands the instant you detect danger.

Watch to see if he retrieves a weapon or if he is about to use his hands as weapons. Let's say that there is a fellow employee in your face shouting about something. Within seconds, he works himself into a screeching teapot, bares his teeth, and draws his hand back to hit. At home, your partner's anger goes from 0 to 60 in a heartbeat. He pushes you against the kitchen counter and draws his fist back to punch.

OPTIONS:

Whether the threat picks up a weapon or cocks his hand, you have three options.

1.   Run. Quickly move back or behind something to avoid the blow, and then run. Distance is your friend. Because of your awareness, you know there is a hall behind you, a door about 10 feet away, an open sidewalk, an exit door in the parking structure. Run hard, and shout, "Leave me alone!"

2.   Shield your head with your arms (see Chapter Six, "Miscellaneous scenarios"). There is no avenue of escape for you or the situation turned violent so quickly that you have only enough time to react by covering yourself. Afterwards, run or attack.

Hunch your shoulders and press your forearms against the side of your head (Photo 1). He might hit you once, twice or three times.

Maintain your shield until there is a moment—he stops, he slips, he loses his balance—in which you can attack him, or run (Photo 2).

3.   Attack like an enraged lioness. When your gut tells you that your best option is to attack—he's slow, he's a stumbling drunk, he reached for a weapon but missed it the first time—you must attack with ferocity.

PREEMPTIVE ATTACK WITH YOUR HANDS

Let's say that you decide that the best defense is to attack first. As mentioned throughout this book, you can hit preemptively only when all indications are that the threat is about to hurt you in some fashion. To reiterate, there must be indications that you're in danger. Hitting him with a preemptive strike when there aren't any is a crime called "assault." You don't need that.

To attack with your hands, you must be able to cross the range with one or two steps. You only get one chance to make a fist impression, so to speak, so it's important to hit a vulnerable target hard. If you can hit that same target more than once, do so. If he turns to avoid or covers himself, hit a different vulnerable target. While this sounds like a no brainer, too often people keep hitting the same target even after the recipient has covered it. Stress and lack of training does that to people.

You deem that the threat is about to attack so you lunge forward (1) with a left-hand claw to his eyes (2), followed by a...

Explode with these techniques: Clawclawkick!

... right-hand claw. You want to claw again but he covers his face.

So you kick his shins instead. Kick multiple times if needed until you can get away.

WATCH OUT FOR HIS FRIENDS

This isn't always an issue at home (though it can be with relatives or your partner's friends), but for sure it can be a problem on the street and in a club. The issue, and it's a common one, is that of tunnel vision. You're so focused on the threat standing before you that you fail to see his buddies who might get involved.

It's not hard to imagine that shooting someone can be an emotional experience like no other. It's easy to be so focused on the target that the officer misses the fact that there are other threats in the vicinity, the bad guy's friends. Therefore, officers train to shoot and scan 360 degrees. They fire at the target, stop shooting, and then before they holster their weapon, they look to their left and right, and behind them. They do this every time they shoot on the firing range until it becomes a natural action.

You should train the same way.

You lunge in with a palm-heel strike once...

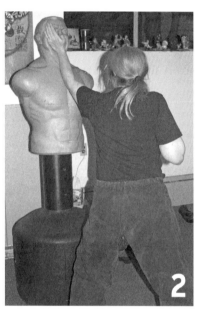

...twice.

As you back away from the threat, quickly look left...

...right (4) and then back at the threat (5). Then flee.

The overall theme of this chapter is that you must function in the Yellow Zone of alertness and awareness the instant you leave your home. If you share your life with an abusive partner, you must function in the Yellow Zone within your home.

How important is mental rehearsal?

It's critical. Way in advance of a conflict you must go over in your head how far you are willing to go and for what reason. That way when you are in a "now or never" moment, you can just move.

■ ■ ■

Once the threat has been detected, and IF the woman has already rehearsed her "line in the sand," then she is much more likely to fight violently.

■ ■ ■

Women have to think about when to activate the "fight trigger before a confrontation. They need to know ahead of time. It's very hard to make this particular decision when the threat is approaching.

■ ■ ■

The women I have had the privilege of teaching have never thought about how a real attack would happen. They don't think about such things. Physical techniques are great, but if the student is not educated on the psychology/mental aspect of an attack, she will freeze from the shock, & horror of it.

■ ■ ■

Mental rehearsal sort of gives you permission to defend yourself. You create a mindset that you will survive and that you are worth defending. It prepares you for the fight.

CHAPTER TEN

MENTAL IMAGERY

Mental imagery, also called visualization and sweatless practice, is a powerful psychological skill used to enhance performance and mental toughness. There is nothing terribly mystical about it. In fact, you already engage in mental imagery whenever you anticipate your involvement in any situation, whether it's giving a presentation at work or planning dinner with friends.

Although the use of mental imagery has a long history in human performance enhancement, it's perhaps best known because of its popularity in high-level athletic competition. For example, 90 percent of the athletes and 94 percent of the coaches surveyed at the United States Olympic Training Center reported that they used imagery.

However, it isn't limited to basketball players and downhill skiers. Today mental imagery is recognized more and more as a powerful training tool for martial artists, military, law enforcement and others who function in the emergency response field. Because people who work on the frontline are quick to abandon anything that does not help them in the gritty world of reality, it's a significant endorsement that mental imagery is rapidly gaining acceptance among them.

"Attention All Units: Armed Robbery in Progress at..."

When Loren was a young cop he patrolled a beat in which there were seven mini-markets: 7-11s, Plaid Pantry's and the like. Cops call these places "Stop-and-robs" because of their popularity among armed robbers. Loren responded to hold-ups once or twice a week. One Christmas eve, gunmen robbed all seven mini markets.

Because armed robberies, especially robbery-in-progress calls, are so dangerous for citizens and officers, Loren spent a few weeks going to each store and studying the best way to approach it by car and on foot, the most likely place the armed robber would flee, the location of backdoors, dumpsters, and the proximity of private homes should there be a shootout. Loren imaged where he would park, where he would take cover should the hold-up man still be on premise, how he would respond if the suspect took a hostage, and what he would do in a number of other "what if" scenarios.

After just two or three weeks of preplanning, all Loren's future responses to this most dangerous call were smooth and as flawless as if he had done it many times before, which he had—in his mind.

Mental Imagery and Self-defense

In short, mental imagery uses your vivid imagination to improve your response in a dangerous situation. For our purposes, think of it as mental rehearsal of the skills you have learned in this book and those you already possess. Before we look at how simple it is to do, here are a few ways this powerful tool benefits you.

SKILL IMPROVEMENT

Mental imagery practice complements and enhances your alertness, situational awareness, deescalating verbal skills, physical skills and your ability to function under great stress. It can be particularly useful with activities that occur one after the other, such as riding your work elevator down to the parking garage, walking to your car in a poorly lit parking structure, unlocking your door, and getting in. By imaging the details of your walk, you ingrain the tools of alertness and awareness. For example:

- you image looking right and left as you exit the elevator.

- you image being alert and aware of everything around you as you make your way to your car.

- you imagine a few large vehicles in the stalls, a large garbage dumpster against a wall, or anything else where someone might hide. You image paying extra attention to them.

- you image someone standing next to a car and you image keeping your eyes on them.

As we shall discuss, the more details you add to your mental imagery, the greater your alertness and awareness when you actually walk from the elevator to your car.

SKILL MAINTENANCE

Even when you cannot practice physically as much as you would like, mental imagery helps you maintain and even improve your proficiency.

War story 1: An American officer held as a prisoner of war passed the time every day playing a round of golf, shot by shot, in his mind. When he went to play for the first time after his release from incarceration, he shot par, despite the rigors of many years in prison and not having played or practiced for all that time. That is, except in his mind.

War story 2: Loren won over 50 trophies during his competitive years in the martial arts.

In one tournament, the Northwest Nationals, he wanted to enter two kata divisions.

Kata is a prearranged set of movements that demonstrate power, speed, perfection of movement, intensity of battle, and other qualities against multiple attackers from multiple angles. Each of Loren's forms consisted of over 100 moves.

Because of time and energy constraints, he decided to physically practice a new kata but use only mental imagery to practice the one he had competed with before. This was a risk because the last two or three months before a big competition he had always practiced daily, as the kata was extremely complex and energy draining. However, Loren wanted to try mental imagery since he had been studying and practicing it for a book he was working on.

On the day of the event, Loren placed 5th place with the kata he had physically practiced and he won 1st place with the one he had only practiced in his mind with mental imagery. In the last event of the day, he competed against all the other black belt winners, using the same kata he had only practiced mentally. He won again, this time the title of overall Grand Champion.

War story 3: Wim Demmere is a martial artist who lives in Belgium where he is a fighting champion and personal trainer. He and Loren have coauthored three books together. Wim is a strong advocate of mental imagery and says this about its effectiveness when he moved up the competition ladder to face tougher and tougher opponents.

"As I was now facing fighters on the international scene, men with knockout power in every technique, I could no longer afford to hold back. So I spent countless hours on mental programming, learning to invoke and then control a powerful mindset. I watched film footage of my fights, mentally reliving each one, imagining going full power where I had held back. My next step was to program my mind and practice deep meditation. I imaged highly detailed fights, each with a different opponent. I imaged fighting them like a demon, not letting up until I'd beaten them unconscious. Although in my mental imagery I was a merciless animal, I made sure I was always in control of my physical actions. Since being out of control is a sure way to lose a fight, it was critical that my mental training included extreme aggression that was in harmony with the right mindset to control it."

ERROR ANALYSIS AND CORRECTION

Let's say that your car is parked at the far end of an open air parking lot. You're tired after a rough day at work as you zigzag your way around vans, jeeps and sedans, as you think about that red blouse you bought on your lunch break at 20 percent off and how good you're going to look in it at the party tonight. You get into your car and just before you turn the key, it occurs to you that you were oblivious to your surroundings all the way across the lot.

It's good that you recognized this error so quickly (too many people remain oblivious) and that you discovered it before you drove off. You can immediately fix this by using mental imagery to redo what just happened. Imaging a better way helps "erase the old tape" of the undesirable and to "reprogram" a more successful response in your brain. It takes about 30 seconds to do.

Here is the easy fix. You can do this with your eyes open or closed. If the area is dangerous, keep them open or leave and do it later.

Before you back out of your slot, image yourself walking across the lot again, this time completely aware of all that is around you (right). Using all your senses, image:

- *walking* in the most open part of the lot.

- *hearing* traffic pass on the street.

- *observing* large vehicles that could be a potential hiding place.

- *seeing* those three teens talking by the brown jeep.

- *feeling* the warm summer wind against your face.

- *seeing* that homeless guy urinating against the back wall.

- *feeling* the keys in your hand.

- *feeling* the weight of your cell phone riding in your closest pocket.

By practicing mental imagery for just 30 seconds, you begin to reprogram yourself to be alert as you walk to your car.

REDUCTION OF SURPRISE AND UNCERTAINTY

When you're surprised by a violent encounter, the shock and your inexperience might delay your response as your mind struggles to interpret the situation and determine a course of action. That one or two seconds might be too long for you to react effectively. However, when you use mental imagery to practice various scenarios, including surprise ones, you condition your brain to respond with greater speed. This is because it recognizes a situation as a dangerous one, which reduces surprise, disbelief and confusion, negative responses that delay an effective defense.

RESPONSE PREPARATION

It's been said that only one thing is certain in combat: something will happen, but it won't be what you prepared for in training. A common saying in the military is: "All training turns to s… after the first shot is fired." But it doesn't have to be that way. Simulation training, in the form of mental imagery, can reduce the surprise factor in an actual situation, resulting in a faster and more effective response.

Let's say that you're imaging your walk across that parking lot and you include someone stepping out from behind another vehicle. The first two or three times you practice, image a nonevent: He walks by you and nods hello (right). This gets you practicing being observant.

Other times image him grabbing your arm (left). Then image your response, one that is explosive and violent. In a real situation, his sudden appearance might still startle you, but because you have perceived him in all your senses before, or someone like him, your surprise will be less intense.

IMAGE CORRECT RESPONSES

Should you mentally rehearse a response sloppily or incorrectly, you will likely perform sloppily or incorrectly in a real situation. It's no different than practicing physically. *How you train is how you perform in a real situation* is an adage quoted by most street oriented martial arts instructors.

While it's important to "see the attacker crumpled on the ground," as emphasized by some instructors when discussing the ultimate goal, we believe the first emphasis should be on the process of getting him down there. We find that imaging dumping him on the ground via the flawless execution of a solid forearm thrust to his neck is more beneficial than simply seeing him already down and writhing. Dr. Mike Mahoney, a pioneer in sport psychology, says that if you focus on the process, the outcome takes care of itself.

IMAGE IN ALL OF YOUR SENSES

As mentioned earlier, some people refer to mental imagery as "visualization." We don't recommend this term because it implies that you image only what you "see" or "visualize." In a real self-defense situation, however, you use all of your senses: sight, hearing, touch, smell and taste. Therefore, your mental rehearsal should include what you would See; what you would Hear; what you would Feel (physical and emotional); what you would Smell; and what you would Taste.

How to do it

Let's look at how to practice this simple procedure. First, here are the steps for the 4-count breathing technique that you use prior to each imagery session. In Chapter Twelve, "Fear," we elaborate on the importance of this breathing technique. For now, here are the steps, each of which takes 4 seconds.

4-COUNT BREATHING TECHNIQUE

1. Breathe in through the nose: 1, 2, 3, 4.

Hold: 1, 2, 3, 4.

Breathe out through the lips: 1, 2, 3, 4.

Hold: 1, 2, 3, 4.

2. Breathe in through the nose:1, 2, 3, 4.

Hold: 1, 2, 3, 4.

Breath out through the lips: 1, 2, 3, 4.

SELF-DEFENSE IN THE NEWS

An 83-year-old woman was loading wood into her fireplace when a man walked into her house through an unlocked sliding door, pushed her face-first into a chair and then pressed himself against her. The woman had read a news story several years earlier, one that she had thought about several times since. It was a story about a woman facing a similar intruder and how she survived by grabbing the man's testicles. So that is what the 83-year-old woman did. The man screamed, tore free and fled. He was arrested a short while later.

Hold: 1, 2, 3, 4.

3. Breathe in through the nose: 1, 2, 3, 4.

Hold: 1, 2, 3, 4.

Breath out through the lips: 1, 2, 3, 4.

Hold: 1, 2, 3, 4.

That is 3 cycles. Don't do less but if you want to do more, that is okay.

Let's being with a scenario in which there are no problems, but there is still a lot going on.

IMAGING A PROBLEM-FREE SCENARIO

Remember, the more vivid, intense, and realistic your imaging, the more you benefit. Let's begin by imaging a walk to your car in a semi-dark parking structure.

Sit in a chair, get comfortable and close your eyes (right). Do at least 3 cycles of the 4-count breathing technique to calm your mind and relax your body.

You may want to have someone read the following instructions to you. If you find that distracting, then memorize the simple steps. Whichever way works for you is fine. After each instruction, image the scene for a few moments, then open your eyes, clear your thoughts, and move on to the next scene. Make each one as vivid as possible, maintain your focus, and don't allow other thoughts to distract you.

In your mind's vision, SEE the parking structure landing as you step out of the elevator. For example, see the low ceiling, cement floor, pavement, round support columns, black exhaust grime on the cement, vehicles of various colors and shapes parked in their spaces, and your car in a slot half way down on the left side.

After a few moments of seeing, open your eyes and clear your mind for a few seconds. Then close your eyes again for the next sense imaging.

In your mind's hearing, HEAR a car start somewhere off to the right and a car honking on the floor below you. Hear your heels clicking on the cement as you walk.

After a few moments of hearing, open your eyes and clear your mind for a few seconds. Then close your eyes again for the next sense imaging.

In your mind's touch, FEEL your steps on the concrete and the weight of your purse on your shoulder.

After a few moments of feeling, open your eyes and clear your mind for a few seconds. Then close your eyes again for the next sense imaging.

In your mind's olfaction, SMELL the exhaust from vehicles moving throughout the parking structure. Can you still smell your perfume at the end of the day? If so, include it.

After a few moments of smelling, open your eyes and clear your mind for a few seconds. Then close your eyes again for the next sense imaging.

In your mind's gustation, TASTE the remains of a mint candy you had earlier and the exhaust wafting throughout the parking structure.

After a few moments of tasting, open your eyes and think about the exercise.

IMAGING A SCENARIO WITH A THREAT

Let's kick it up a notch and add a threat. Not a big kick 'em and punch 'em fight but a threat that you handle with confidence and authority.

Sit in that comfortable chair again, close your eyes and do 3 cycles of the 4-count breathing exercise. Then return to breathing lightly and normally.

Image your walk from the elevator to your car using all of your senses. Think about what you *see*. Think about what you *hear*. Think about what you *feel*. Think about what you *taste*. Think about what you *smell*. You will be imaging some senses several times in this longer session.

In your mind's vision, SEE the parking structure landing as you step out of the elevator: the low ceiling, cement floor, pavement, round support columns, black exhaust grime on the cement, vehicles of various colors and shapes parked in their spaces, and your car half way down the left side. SEE a man standing by a red car parked about four spaces away from you on the left. Is he locking the door or unlocking it? Is it even his car? Is he watching you?

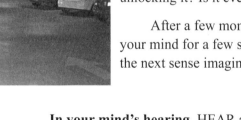

After a few moments of seeing, open your eyes and clear your mind for a few seconds. Then close your eyes again for the next sense imaging.

In your mind's hearing, HEAR a car start somewhere off to the right on the floor and a car honking on the floor below. HEAR your heels clicking on the cement as you walk to your car. HEAR the man say something to you. Was it "Miss?" You don't know.

After a few moments of hearing, open your eyes and clear your mind for a few seconds. Then close your eyes again for the next sense imaging.

In your mind's touch, FEEL your steps on the concrete and the weight of your purse on your shoulder. FEEL your hands slip into your coat pocket and

FEEL your fingers curl around a heavy pen. FEEL your head turn just enough that you can see the man walking in your direction. FEEL a surge of adrenaline flood your body. FEEL your breath quicken a little.

After a few moments of feeling, open your eyes and clear your mind for a few seconds. Then close your eyes again for the next sense imaging.

In your mind's olfaction, SMELL the exhaust of vehicles moving throughout the parking structure at the end of the workday.

After a few moments of smelling, open your eyes and clear your mind for a few seconds. Then close your eyes again for the next sense imaging.

In your mind's gustation, TASTE the remains of a mint candy you had earlier and the exhaust wafting throughout the parking structure.

After a few moments of tasting, open your eyes and clear your mind for a few seconds. Then close your eyes again for the next sense imaging.

In your mind's hearing, HEAR the man's footsteps quicken and grow louder. This time you HEAR "Miss?" more clearly.

After a few moments of hearing, open your eyes and clear your mind for a few seconds. Then close your eyes again for the next sense imaging.

In your mind's touch, FEEL yourself turn around to face him.

After a few moments of feeling, open your eyes and clear your mind for a few seconds. Then close your eyes again for the next sense imaging.

In your mind's hearing, HEAR yourself command him to "STOP right there! Don't come any closer to me."

After a few moments of hearing, open your eyes and clear your mind for a few seconds. Then close your eyes again for the next sense imaging.

In your mind's vision, SEE the man halt in mid-step. Image scanning his body for weapons, SEE his hands empty. Image scanning the area for other people.

After a few moments of seeing, open your eyes and clear your mind for a few seconds. Then close your eyes again for the next sense imaging.

In your mind's hearing, HEAR yourself say in a strong commanding voice, "What do you want? Why are you following me?" HEAR confidence and strength in your voice.

After a few moments of hearing, open your eyes and clear your mind for a few seconds. Then close your eyes again for the next sense imaging.

In your mind's touch, FEEL your hand slip out of your coat pocket, the pen clutched tightly in your hand as you move your arm behind your back.

After a few moments of feeling, open your eyes and clear your mind for a few seconds. Then close your eyes again for the next sense imaging.

In your mind's vision, SEE the man raise his empty palms and his head dip apologetically.

After a few moments of seeing, open your eyes and clear your mind for a few seconds. Then close your eyes again for the next sense imaging.

In your mind's hearing, HEAR him say, "I'm very sorry miss. It's just that I've locked myself out of my car over there and I was hoping you might have a coat hanger so that I can try to open my door."

After a few moments of hearing, open your eyes and clear your mind for a few seconds. Then close your eyes again for the next sense imaging.

In your mind's vision, SEE that his mannerisms appear to be earnest.

After a few moments of seeing, open your eyes and clear your mind for a few seconds. Then close your eyes again for the next sense imaging.

In your mind's hearing, HEAR yourself say, "I don't have one. Now don't follow me anymore."

After a few moments of hearing, open your eyes and clear your mind for a few seconds. Then close your eyes again for the next sense imaging.

In your mind's vision, FEEL yourself in the parking structure, standing firm, radiating confidence (right).

After a few moments of feeling, open your eyes and clear your mind for a few seconds. Then close your eyes again for the next sense imaging.

In your mind's hearing, HEAR the man apologize.

After a few moments of hearing, open your eyes and clear your mind for a few seconds. Then close your eyes again for the next sense imaging.

In your mind's vision, SEE him turn and walk away.

After a few moments of seeing, open your eyes and clear your mind for a few seconds. Then close your eyes again for the next sense imaging.

In your mind's hearing, HEAR his foot steps descend and HEAR yours as you step backward the rest of the way to your car.

After a few moments of hearing, open your eyes and clear your mind for a few seconds. Then close your eyes again for the next sense imaging.

In your mind's vision, SEE the man as he walks back to his car. Image yourself get into your car and lock the door.

After a few moments of seeing, open your eyes, take a breath and shake your muscles a little. Enjoy the good feeling of satisfaction, accomplishment and confidence.

REVIEW

The above imaged situation ended well. It's important to practice those to develop the verbal and physical skills needed to stop a situation before it deteriorates. In a real situation, the man in the parking garage might have been a mugger looking for a weakness in your guard or he might have been someone who legitimately locked his keys in his car. If he was up to no good, your powerful demeanor and strong, commanding voice made him think twice about attacking, at least attacking you. If he really did lock his keys in his car, his approach to asking for help was a thoughtless one; no, make that a dumb one. When they are that dumb, you're under no obligation to be polite.

MAKE YOUR IMAGERY VIVID

This is critical. You want to image as much detail as you can conjure. You want to see it in high-definition 3-D, hear it in surround sound, and smell it in smellovision. If he is a slimy creep, smell his cheap cologne and hair oil. If he is a methamphetamine doper, smell his stench and see his rotten teeth. If he is a drunken ex-partner, image all his traits that you despise. If you image him slapping you, feel the impact and grimace from it. Then feel the surge of savagery fill your muscles with power and speed as you launch into him like an enraged lioness. The more you add to your session the better it fools your brain into thinking that it's real. With time and practice, your brain with believe it *is* a real situation.

USE THE BEST PERSPECTIVE FOR YOU

For our purposes, there are two perspectives for tactical performance imagery.

The external or third person perspective is when you image as if watching (and engaging your other senses) a character in a movie. Some people use this method when they want to remove themselves from the emotion of the situation to analyze it more objectively than is possible when using the internal method. For example, maybe you want to image something that is similar to what happened to you in the past. If the feelings surrounding that event are still intense, imaging it as if seeing yourself on a movie screen might be best.

The internal or first person perspective is when you see, hear, feel, taste and smell what you actually experience during a response.

There are no firm conclusions about which perspective is best for enhancing performance. Recent reports from Olympic athletes note that 17 to 35 percent use internal/first person imagery, 30 to 39 percent use external/third person imagery, and 34 to 44 percent use both.

Dr. Mike Asken's, a police psychologist and Loren's coauthor of *Warrior Mindset* says that his experience working with police, military, athletes and others in areas of human performance has led him "to prefer the internal/ first person perspective, believing that the more realistic view is ultimately important."

USING BOTH PERSPECTIVES

Since both perspectives are effective, consider using both at first. In time, you might settle on one perspective or you might find that you like the variety of both.

Try it this way:

Monday: For 10 minutes, use the external perspective. If you image walking across a parking lot to your car, you will experience it as if you were someone else watching you observe the suspicious man standing outside the dark van.

Wednesday: For 10 minutes, practice that same action from the internal perspective. You perceive the parking lot, dark van and suspicious man from the vantage point of your senses.

Friday: For 10 minutes, use the external perspective as you did on Monday.

The following week, do the internal method on Monday and Friday and the external just on Wednesday. Continue in this fashion until you decide—it might take two weeks or 12—which perspective you think is best for you. Can't decide? No problem. Just continue using both. As we said earlier, some top athletes, cops and soldiers prefer to use both internal and external. What is important is what works best for you.

IMAGE IN REAL TIME

Just as with physical practice, it's useful to begin imaging a skill in slow motion. Ultimately, however, you will image in real-time speed for the best results. Let's say you're imaging a situation where a date has turned violent in the front seat of a car. Your response is to knock the attacker's hand aside, palm-heel strike him in the face three times and then flee from the car.

When you first begin, use slow motion mental imagery to see, feel, taste, smell and hear every minute aspect of the confrontation. If the real situation would take 20 seconds to unfold, your slow motion mental imagery might take 90 seconds. That way you're sure to involve your five senses in every phase. When you're comfortable doing it in slow motion, practice in real time so that you're imaging your offense, defense, and escape in 20 seconds.

Here are several key elements that you want to bring to your real-time imagery.

- Your imagery response should be the same as in a real situation: claw, kick, push, run. Use techniques with which you're comfortable.

- Whenever possible, practice your mental imagery in the environment in which you're concerned that you might have a problem: parking garage, your car, living room, on a jogging trail.

- Focus your imaged attention on the same thing that would concern you in an actual situation: weapons, the way your partner attacked in the past, avenues of escape, and so on.

- Incorporate emotions—fear, anxiety, anger, hate—in your mental imagery.

- Use whatever perspective—internal, external—works best for you.

ADD MINI MOVEMENTS TO YOUR IMAGERY

While mental imagery is a psychological technique, it does not mean you have to be perfectly still or passive when practicing. You can employ small motions that mimic, in part, the skills that you're imaging. You will not move at full speed and intensity, and you will not fully extend your arms and legs. Instead, you gently move your limbs or torso about three inches, 12 at the most, just enough to add a sense of "feel" with the imagery.

We enjoy tai chi, the Chinese martial art easily recognized by its ultra slow movements. A typical form involves moving forward, backward, diagonally, to the sides, and in a circle, all the while executing fighting movements that appear

to be floating in the air. Sometimes we practice tai chi sitting or standing in place with mental imagery. When we include mini movements, we move our arms just a little when striking, our upper body a little when turning, and our legs a little when stepping and kicking. The motions are so small and subtle that an onlooker would have no idea what we are doing. In our mind, however, our arms are extending fully, our bodies are turning completely, and our footwork is completed.

Here is how you can use mini movements to image a brief physical confrontation. In realty, the situation as presented here would take about 30 seconds, which means your imagery should last just as long. When imaging for five minutes, you can easily complete eight to ten imaged repetitions. You don't need to change into sweats and you will not need to shower after. You don't even have to get out of your chair. Here is how it's done:

1. Sit in a comfortable chair, close your eyes and bring on a sense of relaxation using the 4-count breathing technique. In this exercise, you flow from image to image without pausing to absorb the sensory perceptions.

2. Image: You're in your kitchen preparing a meal for your partner. If you usually have music on or a television playing, hear those sounds as well as the sounds of chopping vegetables. Using very small hand motions, mimic chopping with a knife. See your hand holding the stalk of celery and chopping it with the other. SMELL something cooking in the oven or on a hotplate.

3. Image: HEAR your partner coming into the house and do what he does when he is in a terrible mood or has been drinking. Maybe he curses because the TV is on or complains because the dinner is not ready. HEAR his complaints and FEEL the agitation his words create in your body. Turn your torso three or four inches in your chair to mimic turning to SEE him enter the kitchen.

4. Image: Set the knife on the cutting board and wipe your hands on a towel as you HEAR his grumbling. Pantomime these actions using small movements with your hands and arms. If his actions normally upset your stomach or make your heart beat rapidly, FEEL that in your body. SEE his angry face and HEAR his insulting words.

5. Image: SEE him get more upset no matter what words you use to calm him—you can speak the words aloud or HEAR them in your mind—and FEEL the adrenaline in your body surge throughout your muscles. Straighten your posture in your chair and feel yourself stand taller as you face him.

6. Image: FEEL yourself step back until your back touches the counter, physically move your legs and feet minutely at the same time. FEEL your hands lift up to your chest. Fiddle with your blouse, lightly fold your arms or do anything else to position your hands so you can quickly defend yourself.

7. Image: SEE him step toward you in anger. FEEL the anxiety this causes and then FEEL yourself physically relax your body. Your hands are still near

your chest. FEEL the energy and power in your body. FEEL the confrontation charge your body with readiness. FEEL these things supersede any anxiety or fear you might have. Say aloud, or in your mind, "Leave me alone!" "Get back!"

8. Image: SEE his right, open hand draw back and shoot rapidly toward your face in an arc. FEEL your left forearm shoot up to cover the side of your face. Physically lift your left arm a little. If you want, lift it all the way up and actually shield your face.

9. Image: SEE and FEEL his hand make contact with your arm. Physically, react as if actually struck.

You can add any number of conclusions. You can counter-hit him with a body weapon and flee the house; you can push him against the oven or refrigerator and flee; or you can run from the house without responding at all. Consider imaging different response. For one session, image hitting him with a pot; the next session, image pushing him away from you; and for the next one, image running like mad after you block his slap. For now, push him into something.

10. Image: FEEL yourself give him a mighty push into the corner of the door facing. Physically, push with your hands and arms using small movements, and drive with your legs by moving your thighs and feet ever so slightly. Contract all the muscles in your body as you mentally slam him with all the prejudice you can conjure.

11. Image: FEEL your feet step forward and smash his neck with a hammerfist before he can push away from the doorway.

"Chair pantomiming" is another term for what you just did. Now let's look at standing pantomiming in which you execute the techniques with full motions.

PANTOMIME FULL MOVEMENTS WHEN IMAGING

You don't have to dress like a mime and wear white face, but if it helps…

Pantomiming full movements work best right after you have physically practiced with a partner. Let's say that you and your partner have been practicing defense against an arm grab. He grabs you, you step into the pull, slam your shin into his groin and follow with a palm-heel strike to his face. The two of you practice this for 15 minutes.

As soon as you get home and before you hit the shower, pantomime the sequence 5 to 10 times while it's still fresh in your mind. Here is the caveat: You do it with your eyes closed. This way you can better:

- SEE the techniques.

- FEEL the techniques as you execute them and FEEL your balance (or lack of it) as you move about.

- HEAR the exhalation of your breath as you image the impact of your

blows.

- SMELL whatever you can smell in the place in which you're pantomiming. While smelling might not affect the quality of your techniques, it contributes to the realism of your mental imaging experience.

- TASTE whatever you taste: gum, Lifesaver, toothpaste, old onions from lunch. Tasting also contributes to the realism of your mental imaging experience.

So before you take a shower close your eyes and image your arm grabbed by an attacker. Image realizing that his grip is too strong; you cannot pull away. Without hesitation, slam your lower shin up and into his groin. (Kicking with your eyes closed might throw you off balance. The more you practice, the better it gets.) Image setting your foot down and flowing into a palm-heel strike to his face.

You don't have to pantomime fast but you still want to experience every sensory aspect of the technique as if you were doing it fast. While all senses are important in your mental imagery, your sense of feel is especially significant.

- FEEL him pulling your arm: his grip on your wrist, how the pull jerks your shoulder, neck and torso.

- FEEL the muscles in your lower body take an adjustment step when you're pulled.

- FEEL the muscles in your leg contract when you lift your leg and slam your shin into his groin as if trying to drive the center of his interest up to his chin.

- FEEL your balance control your leg as you return it to the floor.

- FEEL your hip rotate as you thrust your palm up and into his jawbone.

- FEEL the impact on your palm.

Strive to feel everything you can as you pantomime in the darkness of your closed eyes.

Free tip: Do it in a space free of things that might stub your toe, bang your shinbone, or stumble yourself out an open window.

HOW MUCH SHOULD YOU PRACTICE?

There is no definitive answer as to how much imagery practice you need for maximum performance. About a fifth of Olympic athletes use it every day and nearly half use it three to five days a week. One piece of research shows that to obtain the best results one should practice imagery in sessions lasting three to fifteen minutes.

A FEW ROUTINES

Here are a few ways to train with mental imagery as described in this chapter.

METHOD: 1

You have just trained with a friend practicing five defensive and offensive techniques. Afterwards, you go home and before you take a shower, you close your eyes and pantomime all five moments 5 times each. Use full body movements and full extension with your arms and legs. This should not take longer than 5 to 8 minutes. Now hit the shower.

Afterwards, sit down in your favorite chair and do 3 cycles of the 4-count breathing exercise. Once you feel calm and relaxed, go through the five movements using mental imagery and mini-movements. Do each technique 5 times, which should take 5 minutes.

METHOD 2:

You train with a partner as in Method 1 and then do standing pantomime only.

METHOD 3:

You train with a partner as in Method 1, but afterwards you practice only seated imagery with mini-movements.

METHOD 4:

You have not been able to physically train for a while so you maintain your skill with pantomime practice and seated mini-movements at least twice a week, three times preferred. Choose about 5 techniques and do each one—pantomiming and mini-movements—10 times per session.

METHOD 5:

You're unable to physically practice with a live human so you must practice on your own. Choose 5 techniques (more if you have been training for a while and can comfortably handle a higher volume) and physically practice them in the air in front of a full-length mirror. Then close your eyes and pantomime them—5 times each—using all your

Combining practice

Practice moving meditation as soon as possible after training with a live opponent so that all that you saw and felt is still fresh in your mind. Say you did 50 reps with your training partner, 25 pantomiming imagery reps in the air, and 25 partial-movement mental imagery reps in your easy chair. When you train with attention to every small facet in all three training methods, your mind (and body) believes that you actually performed all 100 reps with a partner.

In a way, you did.

senses. Take your shower. Then plop into your favorite chair, close your eyes and induce relaxation using the 4-count breathing technique. Now practice your mental imagery using mini-movements.

METHOD 6:

Sometimes you might want to get in a little imagery practice for a few minutes without inducing relaxation via 4-count breathing. Will this be as effective as the more formal versions? Probably not. Will it still make you a little bit better than if you did nothing? Yes.

Here are three situations in which you can practice:

In the shower: Perhaps you like to let the shower beat down on your back for a few seconds. Instead of singing and scaring your pets, close your eyes and see and feel yourself, say, block a face slap and return one of your own. The whole thing should take 2 seconds. Image it 10 times.

In your car: You're waiting to pick up your kid at school. Close your eyes and image someone yanking open your car door. Feel your body lean away from the reaching hand and see your leg kick at the attacker's groin. See him stumble back, and see and feel your hands and arms pull the door shut and lock it. That takes about 8 seconds. Image it 5 to 10 times.

Standing in line: You're waiting in line at the grocery. Put down the tabloid newspaper and stand behind your cart with your hands on its push bar. Keep your eyes open and focus on a can of soup in your cart. Image someone standing next to your car as you push the cart out to your parking spot. Decide what you're going to do and image it.

You will no doubt find other methods as you practice over the next few weeks and months. Practicing moving mental imagery and practicing imagery without moving are powerful ways to ingrain quality technique into your memory. Doing it more casually, such as standing in line, sitting in your car, and showering is also valuable but not to the same extent as standing and partial movements. In the end, however, it all adds up to making you the best you can be.

Lt. Col. Dave Grossman, with whom Loren wrote the bestseller *On Combat*, says that the important goals of military training are to take the surprise out of combat, raise the sense of confidence, and cognitively prepare the warrior for battle. Mental imagery, when integrated with other physical skill training, contributes to reaching these goals.

Comment more on mental imagery . . .

If a woman has addressed the use of force and has been taught how to carry herself, how to avoid dangerous situations, and how to fine-tune her awareness skills, she is far less likely to be victimized.

■ ■ ■

You can learn all the self-defense you want, but if you are scared to death, it's useless. You must prepare mentally as well.

■ ■ ■

Women have a 6th sense about themselves and people around them that is more powerful than a man's ability. Mental training enhances this.

■ ■ ■

Women need to work through how they feel about fighting, and what they would fight for and why, so that when they have to fight, they can give themselves permission to act decisively in the moment. They can't afford the hesitation that we would naturally feel to engage and cause harm.

CHAPTER ELEVEN

MENTAL IMAGERY ON LIVE PEOPLE

This powerful way to practice mental imagery is part imagination and part "live attackers." The live attackers might be waiting for the bus with you, standing in line ahead of you at the movies, walking past you on the sidewalk, or feeding pigeons in the park as you pass. In reality, they are innocent people minding their own business and paying you no mind. Still, you're going to image palm-heel striking them in the face, kicking them in the groin, pushing them to the ground, and using their eyeballs as a scratching post.

Some readers might argue that this is sick. We argue that it's excellent training. In a perfect world, you would not have to think this way, but the fact that the world can be an insane and dangerous place makes this easy-to-access and easy-to-do training necessary.

Police officers use this, and so do our military and our top athletes. Loren taught it to officers in the police academy and to regulars in in-service training, and always received excellent feedback from those who implemented it. He learned it from Chuck Norris who used it in his competition years to image fighting a competitor he had never before faced in the ring.

Norris watched how the fighter clashed with other opponents: how he moved, stood, kicked and threw punches. Then Norris imaged how he would respond to the man offensively and defensively in the ring. By imaging in this fashion, Norris gave himself a huge advantage when he actually faced the fighter in competition. While it was his opponent's first time to face Norris, Norris had the advantage of having fought the man many times before, albeit in his mind. Did it work? Chuck Norris was the middleweight champion of the world before his movie career took off.

Mental imagery training on live people is something you do occasionally. That said, at first you might want to do it often, say, once or twice a day. It only takes a few seconds and it can be fun, in a sick sort of way.

Read this:

A man standing by the apple display in the grocery reaches to the top of the pile with his right hand—*you side stomp kick his right, outer thigh*—picks one up and puts it into his cart.

It took you about three or four times longer to read the above sentence than it would take to image kicking the shopper's thigh. Your kick—chamber, kick, retract and return to the floor—would take two seconds at the most.

The beauty of this is that no one knows you're doing it (unless you let out a karate yell in the middle of the aisle).

Here is another example: You're in your break room when your boss comes in to pour himself a cup of coffee. He nods and asks, "How's it going today?"

You look up, smile and mentally kick him in the groin with your shinbone. "Doing fine, sir. Just enjoying a moment."

"Good, good, good," he says in that way bosses do, and leaves with his cup. To your amazement, he is walking normally.

A student once asked if she concentrated hard enough would the target of her mental imagery actually feel her attack. We're guessing no, but stranger things have happened.

Practicing this way a few times a day helps you to:

- recognize opportunities.

- recognize targets.

- recognize pathways to targets.

- choose the right technique for the occasion.

- choose the right moment to attack.

- maintain a state of alertness and awareness.

TOTAL STRANGERS

Let's examine a few photos that represent typical images that you see everyday. Examine them for the following:

- Which open targets do you see?

- Which targets are the most vulnerable?

- Which weapon in your arsenal is the best one for the target?

- Which weapon in your arsenal would be a good option?

- Which weapon in your arsenal would slow him enough for you to escape?

- Which weapon in your arsenal would debilitate him?

- Which angle would you use to hit the target?

- What is the likely result of hitting a specific target?

There is much to learn by looking at a person and pondering what you could do if you were defending yourself against him.

Let's begin by examining the first pic at right.

Can you see which targets are open and how his weight is distributed? A person standing in this manner is a relatively easy target. Let's start at the top and work down.

Look Beyond the Subject

As we talk about in Chapter Five, "Weapons, weapons everywhere," the world is one big weapons cache. On an average day, there are enough weapons around you to wipe out a half dozen Nazis.

Therefore, when you look at your target—that man reading the paper in the bus aisle, the biker chick in line at Starbucks, the man in the thousand dollar suit waiting at the car wash—include in your attack all available weapons. By the time you conclude your five-second mental imagery attack on the hapless person, you will have kicked, punched, elbowed, hit him with your bag from Macy's, and clobbered him with an orange traffic cone. Practice in this manner for a week and you will be amazed at how quickly you're able to choose what to use in your defense.

- Head:
  - palm-heel strike his forehead, nose, ears, and jawbone.
  - hammerfist his nose, forehead, ears.
  - claw his eyes, mouth and ears.
  - elbow strike his eyes, nose and ears.
  - slap his cheeks, nose, and ears.

- Neck:
  - hammerfist all four sides.
  - elbow strike all four sides.
  - slap the front of his throat.

- Upper body
  - palm-heel his chest to keep him back.
  - elbow his solar plexus to knock the wind out of him.
  - claw his nipples to make him scream.

- Pelvis area
  - elbow his bladder and groin.
  - hammerfist his bladder and groin.
  - kick his bladder and groin.

- Legs:
  - hammerfist the peroneal nerve on the outside of his leg.
  - kick his peroneal nerve, the inside of his thighs, knees, and shins.

- Feet:
  - kick his ankle bones and Achilles tendon.
  - stomp the top of his foot and toes.

Did you realize that you knew so many ways to attack?

All targets from the top of his head to his feet that were present in the first photo are open and ready to attack in this one. However, he has raised his arm and shifted his weight to his right leg. The raised arm is obvious but his weight change is less so. If you noticed, good for you. If you didn't, or you did but failed to realize its importance, no problem. You will. Did you see his raised hand as more than just a wave? Good job if you imaged it as the beginning of a slap. If you didn't, you will next time.

Here is how to image it for your self-defense training. Say you're sitting in your car waiting for the light to change. You glance over to the sidewalk and see a man raise his hand to wave to someone across the street. Image the following in first person:

- see the man.

- see the man raise his arm to wave.

- imagine that it's a slap attack.

- see and feel yourself lower your body for stability.

- see and feel yourself shield block the left side of your face with your left arm.

- see and feel yourself thrust your shielding block hand into his face and claw your nails downward.

- see and feel yourself thrust your right claw hand into his face and shred downward.

- see and feel yourself push both of your palms against his chest in the direction of his right leg.

- see him grab at his face as he falls to his right.

- see and feel yourself turn and flee.

That bit of mental imagery took two or three seconds tops. As you drive off, enjoy the fact that you:

- saw the arm gesture.

- imagined it to be a threat.

- responded defensively.

- countered offensively.

- avoided a nasty blow to your face.

Your secret

As mentioned before, practicing imagery might seem strange to you at first, something so far out of your norm that it frightens you. Some women have said that it's upsetting, others say that they wish things were different so that they didn't have to practice this at all. That is a normal thought and understandable, but don't let that stop you from practicing it. Wishful thinking will not help you in a violent confrontation.

Practicing for it will.

Again, all the previous targets are open. What is different in this pic is that Loren has lifted one foot. Use your imagination to modify the image to fit your mental scenario. Could he be kicking someone, a friend, a relative? Might he be stepping down from his truck after threatening you? Might he be kicking the side of your car door?

Can you see how weak his balance is? It would not take much of a push to send him stumbling or even crashing to the cement. See and feel your right, lower shin slam into his groin, not once, but twice. Set your foot down and ram your supported forearm into his chest in the direction of his right leg. See him crumple to the cement as you turn and run off.

You see a man tying his shoe. Image that he has swung at you, missed, and lost his balance. Or image him with his hands on the floor pushing his way back up. There are fewer targets available in this picture, but you can still:

- kick his shin.

- kick his forearm or hand.

- kick his head.

- grab a wad of hair and pull him down.

Write the following on a post-it and stick it on your bathroom mirror: *No matter what position an attacker is in, there is always a target available somewhere.*

As you walk from your car toward a grocery store, you see a man walking in your direction. Image that he is a threat. For example, imagine that he just shouted that he is going to get you. What would you do at this distance?

- Wait until he gets close enough to fight?

- Run?

Most often, running is the best choice at this range—as long as you know in which direction you're going. Logical? Not to everyone. We know of two people who, in blind panic, dashed away from a threat, one slammed into a tree and the other into the side of a truck. As we have said throughout this book, know where you are and what is around you, especially the location of potential weapons and avenues of escape.

Two or three times a week, pretend that the person walking toward you is a threat, whether it's man, woman or child. Ask yourself, without cheating and looking around: Where could I run? If you have been practicing awareness, you will answer instantly. If you haven't, well, be thankful it's not a real situation.

As you walk across a parking lot, you see this man, Pic A, passing by the trunk of your car. Let your imagination run wild and imagine him to be a threat. What would you do considering how far away he is?

- Circle around the front of the car?

- Step behind a car fender to create distance?

- Run?

- Confront him?

- Find something to use as a weapon on your person or in your purse?

Think deeply about your answers. Imagine articulating them to another person.

Let's say that you don't see the man until you're as close to him as pictured in Pic B. Again, imagine that he is a threat to you.

- Do you still have time to run?

- Can you still retrieve a weapon?

- Can you still call out for help?

- Can you circle around the front of the car?

- Do you have your keys in your hand?

- Can you step behind a car fender to create distance?

- What targets are available to hit?

- Can you shout: "Leave me alone!" "Someone help me!" "Someone call 9-1-1!"?

Think deeply about your answers. Imagine articulating them to another person?

Lock your doors immediately when you get into your car. Too many women get in and sit for a moment updating their checkbooks or searching for the best CD. Do that after you lock your car doors.

Let's say you're sitting in your car at a stop sign and you see a man crossing the street off to your side. Allowing your imagination to run wild, ask yourself what you would do if he were charging toward you from the distance in Pic A.

- Is there time for you to drive off?

- Is there time for you to roll up your window, lock your doors and blow your horn?

- Is there time for you to retrieve a weapon from your purse or inside your car?

If you were first in line at a red light or stop sign, you might be able to make a fast right turn. If the light is red and there are no cars coming, you can make a left (don't worry about it being illegal). If you're two or three cars back at the stop, you might be able to turn into a right turn lane. As always, be aware so you know what to do in an instant.

In Pic B, the threat is only a stride or two away from your window.

- Is there time to drive off?

- Is there time to roll up your window and lock your door?

- Is there time to retrieve a weapon from your purse or inside your car?

- Can you lean on your horn?

- Can you push your door into him?

Road rage

Many road rage incidents happen like this: You accidentally cut someone off and the driver honks and flips you a one-finger salute. Twenty minutes later you get to your destination only to discover that the violated driver, madder than a wet hornet, has been following you.

Road ragers share these common traits: Their tempers are volatile and their violent actions are out of proportion to the perceived violation.

Be alert. Be aware.

The close proximity of the threat changes things. You probably don't have enough time to roll up your window, but you do have time to lock your door and lean on the car horn. You might not have enough time to turn into another lane but you do have enough time to grab a weapon from your door pocket—screwdriver, wrench, hammer—to attack his reaching hands.

There were a couple times when Loren was a cop when he used his car door to slam into the legs of a person who was trying to attack him through the window. It was if Detroit had slamming a car door into an assailant's shins in mind when they designed the cars. Both times the recipients yelped in agony and jumped around clutching their injured legs.

You're getting out of you car at work when you see a man getting out of his. You imagine that he is a road rager coming after you.

Things to consider:

- Is there time and space for you to run?

- Where would you run?

- Is he armed?

- Do you have a weapon?

- Should you jump back in your car and lean on the horn?

- Should you attack him first?

Does he have a weapon? If it's a firearm, do what he says. If it's anything else, running is probably your best choice.

If he is just three or four feet away when you see him getting out, and you have no escape route, attacking him first might be your best option. You need to be justified, of course. If he is growling that he's going to hurt you in some fashion, and his demeanor indicates that he is angry, that is probably enough justification for you to attack first so that you can flee. We say "probably" because you never know how things will go in court.

War story: Loren was working the front desk at the downtown police precinct one quiet day when two men, one chasing the other, burst through the glass doors and crashed to the floor in a tangle of flailing fists and feet. Officers pounced on them quickly and pulled them apart. When the dust settled, the police learned that the man pursuing was a road rager from a confrontation that began a block up the street. The victim had deliberately run to the police station seeking help. The other man was in such a rage that he failed to notice the police cars out front, and the large sign: POLICE PRECINCT.

This time you're not imaging a live person who crosses your path but rather a photograph. Here we have a typical tourist photo (Loren with his head shaved). You cannot pull his hair but look at all the other targets. You can even image pushing him into Washington DC's Reflecting Pool. Use photos in magazines, books, and moving images on television and in the movies for your mental imagery practice.

The more you do this the easier it gets. It's all about rehearsing for a real scenario by learning to recognize threats, considering environments, thinking about targets, recognizing environmental weapons, and looking for avenues of escape.

PERSON OF CONCERN

Perhaps there is a person of concern in your life, such as an abusive husband or volatile boyfriend. Until you can get away for good, you must be vigilant around him, especially careful about what you say and do so that you don't set him off. Take every opportunity to rehearse mentally.

Do it two ways:

- Put the person of concern's face on a total stranger.

- Image on the person of concern.

SUPERIMPOSE YOUR SUBJECT'S FACE ON A STRANGER'S FACE:

When you see someone crossing the street toward you, getting out of a car, or reading a magazine at a newsstand, superimpose the person's face you're concerned about over the stranger's face. Then do as you did in the last section on live people: Image running if you have an escape route, slamming him with the car door, kicking his shin, clawing his eyes and doing anything else that fits into the brief moment that you're looking at him.

PRACTICE ON YOUR PERSON OF CONCERN:

Never pass up an opportunity to practice imagery on the very person you're concerned about: your spouse, your alcoholic brother, the office creep, your former best friend, or the weirdo you dated a couple weeks ago. You know how the person of concern walks, sits, stands, and how he becomes so easily upset. If this person has attacked you in the past with a kick, slap, or push, know that people tend to repeat actions that have worked for them before.

Watch him as he moves about you. When he stands, scan his available targets. When he reaches for something, imagine blocking his arm and clawing his face. Image pushing him down when he stands off balance. When he bends over, image grabbing his hair and yanking him down to the floor.

Practicing in this fashion creates familiarity in your mind so that in reality, blocking his slap, ramming your forearm into his neck and stomping on his toes is something that you have already done, albeit just in your mind.

As noted in the beginning of this chapter, mental imagery is a powerful tool used by Olympic athletes, police officers and the military. They use it for one reason: It works.

What do you teach about fear?

Threaten someone we love and we will draw on the inner warrior we didn't know we had to protect them. Women move to "no holds barred" very quickly when our loved ones are threatened. We need to develop the same willingness to protect ourselves as we have for protecting others.

■ ■ ■

Empowerment and strength inevitably come from within. We must have inner strength to be able to draw on physical strength. Inner strength often shows outwardly and, for a woman, might prevent the need to defend herself.

■ ■ ■

Men have "rules of engagement." Even in a barroom brawl, a slap would be "unfair" and biting or scratching unheard of. But a woman will do whatever is necessary to compensate for her lack of size or strength. It takes a lot to get women to the point of fighting, but I believe that even the gentlest woman would gouge eyes, rip testicles, and tear flesh if she felt her children were in danger.

■ ■ ■

Learn to defend yourself in every way possible. Confidence helps you control fear but it has to be confidence that based on self-knowledge of your ability to take care of business.

■ ■ ■

Every time I feel apprehension or fear, I put in some extra training.

■ ■ ■

It's not about ridding fear, but using it.

CHAPTER TWELVE

The Gift of Fear

FEAR

Fear is a topic worthy of an entire book but space limits us to suggesting only a few highly effective techniques that have worked for female and male students. To delve more deeply into the subject, we highly recommend Gavin de Becker's book *Gift of Fear* as an excellent resource for women. His other books—*Fear Less, Just 2 seconds*, and *Protecting the gift*—are excellent as well, but *Gift of Fear* is directly applicable to the subject matter of this book.

As children, our parents told us not to be afraid, as did our grandparents and teachers; our friends teased us if we were. But fear exists to keep us safe and to keep us from doing foolish things, such as kicking over outlaw bikers' motorcycles and jogging on the freeway. We don't want to eliminate fear; we want to control it and function in it.

What follows in this chapter are simple techniques that have worked for our students and us. Since we all have different histories and specific needs, there is not one technique that works for everyone. It's often said that a cowardly woman and a brave woman both feel fear. The difference is that the brave woman controls her fear and the cowardly woman is controlled by it. What follows are simple techniques to help you control yours.

A proven breathing technique

World War II General SLA Marshall said, "Fear in combat is ever present, but it is uncontrolled fear that is the enemy." Perhaps the first step in controlling your fear is to control your thinking, which controls your body and mind. The 4-count breathing technique, mentioned several times in this book, will help you achieve this. You have to breathe anyway, even when you're frightened, so here is a way to do it that helps control your body, mind, and ultimately your actions. In the bestselling book *On Combat* by Lt. Col. Dave Grossman and Loren, they describe the following way to practice this powerful breathing technique.

There is still a need for extensive research to see how long each phase should be held, but for many years now, the 4-count method has worked wonders for warriors around the globe. Once you start using it, you can tailor it to your body's needs. For example, you might find that you need to hold each count for five seconds and that you need five cycles of the procedure to achieve the desired effect. This is fine. It is like adjusting a tuning knob: Grab hold of the knob and keep tuning it until you get "dialed in" to the level that works for you. For now, let us use the 4-count method. Begin by breathing in through your nose to a slow count of four, which expands your belly like a balloon. Hold for a count of 4, and then slowly exhale through your lips for a count of 4, as your belly collapses like a balloon with its air released. Hold empty for a count of 4 and then repeat the process. That is it. Short, but effective.

Now, follow along as we guide you through the procedure.

In through the nose 2, 3, 4. Hold 2, 3, 4. Out through the lips 2, 3, 4. Hold 2, 3, 4.

In through the nose 2, 3, 4. Hold 2, 3, 4. Out through the lips 2, 3, 4. Hold 2, 3, 4.

In through the nose 2, 3, 4. Hold 2, 3, 4. Out through the lips 2, 3, 4. Hold 2, 3, 4.

Maybe you are feeling a little mellow now or maybe you didn't notice a difference since you were already relaxed. But in a life and death situation, we know this simple exercise can be a true revolution in human development. For the first time in human history, we are teaching large portions of our population to consciously control the unconscious part of their body.

Besides slowing your heart rate, and lowering your pulse rate and blood pressure, the 4-count breathing technique calms your body and mind so that you can think better to react physically with control.

Use this breathing technique:

- whenever you feel stressed, anxious or fearful.
  - you're in a dangerous part of town; you heard something outside your home; you're about to take public transportation.
- minutes before your angry partner gets home.
  - he called you earlier enraged about something; you know he has been out drinking.
- as you walk through that dark parking structure.
  - there have been car break-ins, purse snatches and muggings.
- when you think something is about to happen.
  - your spouse is yelling at you in another room; there are several street kids around the store entry.
- to calm yourself in the middle of a situation.
  - your partner has been verbally abusive and leaves the room for a moment; an enraged customer leaves for a moment.
- to calm yourself after a violent situation.
  - you clashed with your partner and he has left; you're waiting for the police after defending yourself against a mugger.

The 4-count breathing technique is a versatile tool used by our military and police agencies before going into harm's way. Martial arts students use it to calm themselves before a match or a test. These people use it because it works.

It's okay to be afraid

The first step toward controlling fear is to *admit that you're afraid.* Men have a more difficult time doing this than women because, well, they are men, and partly because many believe that to admit their fear means that they cannot cope with it. Wrong. Admitting it, as least to yourself, is a simple acknowledgment of what you're experiencing. Acceptance of its existence can help you think clearly and help you work through the source of your fear so that you respond in a real situation as you have trained.

Accepting your fear does not mean that you focus your thinking on the danger or that you might get hurt. Negative thinking takes up valuable space where positive thinking should reside, making it impossible to think about the successful outcome of a confrontation. Instead, recognize that you're afraid and then apply one of the following techniques so that you can do what needs to be done.

What-if questions

Because what-if questions relate to fear of the unknown, it's critical that you respond to each one that arises within you. The greater the clarity and detail in your answers, the less trepidation you're likely to have. Here are a few typical what-if questions that women have.

"What if a man is hiding over there behind that tree?"

"What if there is someone lying down in my backseat?"

"What if my husband comes home drunk and angry?"

"What if something happens when my kids are with me?"

"What if I get hurt?"

These important questions need answering. To get you started, consider the following answers. Notice that most of them refer to material that appears in this book, while others are common sense. As simple as these answers are (feel free to insert more), think about them deeply so that you completely understand how you would respond. It's important that the questions and the answers apply to you, your situation and your lifestyle.

What-if: "What if a man is hiding over there behind that tree?"

Your answer: I will keep my distance from the tree; I will be in the Red Zone; I will arm myself with something from my purse; I will have an avenue of escape; I will know where my cell phone is.

What-if: "What if there is someone lying down in my backseat?"

Your answer: I will look through the back window and then the side windows before I get in; I will arm myself with something from my purse; I will know where my cell phone is.

What-if: What if my husband comes home drunk and angry tonight?"

Your answer: I will go to a friend's house; I will try to calm him; I will *not* let him hit me; I *will* fight back; I know where things are in each room that I can use as a weapon.

What-if: "What if something happens when my kids are with me?"

Your answer: I will be mindful of always being in the Yellow Zone of alertness and awareness; I will know who is around us at all times; I will know the location of escape routes; I will know where my cell phone is; I will fight like an animal to protect them; no one will harm my kids.

What-if: "What if I am hurt?"

Your answer: It's just pain and it will go away; I will fight back no matter how badly I'm hurt; I won't allow a !$%^&* piece of !$%^& to get the best of me; I *will* keep fighting no matter what happens; I *will* survive; I WILL SURVIVE.

WHEN-THEN SENTENCES

Another way to respond to what-if questions is to rephrase them into "When-Then" sentences.

"When my husband comes home drunk and angry, then I will____"

"When I see someone watching me intently as I walk to my car, then I will__"

"When something happens and my kids are with me, then I will___"

By removing the what-if structure, you remove fear of the unknown and add a plan of action that helps alleviate the sense of helplessness that is inherent in the question format.

Focus on your attack

Once the threat has crossed your predetermined line where you will either fight or flee, your task is to focus on what you need to do to end the confrontation. If it's to physically defend yourself, your focus must burn like a laser beam to stop the threat so you can get away. It's about kicking, shoving, clawing, striking with your hands, elbows, shins, forearms, and with any and all environmental weapons.

To paraphrase World War II General Douglas MacArthur (we've changed his gender reference): *The courageous woman is the woman who, in spite of her fear, forces herself to carry on.* You must use your fear and the cause of it—an abusive partner, aggressive bar patron, street mugger—to motivate you to do what needs to be done. Think of the fear in your chest as rocket fuel that charges and motivates you to fight like a lioness protecting its cubs. Just as that cat will not give up until the threat to its babies is gone, you too must fight until the attacker is on the ground, he has run off, or you're able to flee.

Reread the story about the 51-year-old nurse, Susan Kuhnhausen at the beginning of this book. The hired hitman punched her, thrashed all over the floor with her, and hit her in the head with a hammer—but she did not give up. She

SELF-DEFENSE IN THE NEWS

The 27-year-old woman suspected trouble the minute she pulled her pizza deliver vehicle in front of the dark house. Two young men approached her passenger door, one of them removing money from his pocket. She got out with the pizza.

One of them teased her about being scared, and then pulled out a silver handgun and stuck it in her face. She handed him $19 and her car keys but the gunman wanted her to get into the trunk. She refused.

When the second man tried to force her in, she resisted and said she had a one-year-old baby at home. The man with the gun said he didn't care and then he shot her in the thigh.

She later said that she knew right then that the two were willing to do a lot more. That is when she decided to "take him out."

First, she put the bullet wound out of her mind. Then she grabbed the gunman by his wrist, threw him to the ground, and pried the weapon out of his hand. When the other man jumped on her back, she pointed the gun over her shoulder and at his face, pulled the trigger, but the weapon jammed.

When she tried to clear it, the man chomped onto her elbow until she released the gun. He stood up and tried to pull her up by her shirt, but she "went dead weight on him."

She told him, "You can have the shirt off my back, you can have everything in my pockets but I'm not getting in the trunk." He tried to pull the trigger again but the gun was still jammed.

The men finally gave up and drove off in her car.

Later, the woman said that she is taking a break from delivering pizzas but she is not going to let the incident change her. "He thought I was going to roll over but he picked the wrong one," she said of the shooter. "I'm not afraid now and I'm not going to be afraid tomorrow."

ignored her injuries and stayed the course until the hitman was no longer a threat. That kind of focus, that kind of ferocity, uses fear to fuel the lioness that resides within you.

Loren knows of a police officer who works in one of the most violent sections of an East Coast city. People die there on the sidewalks every week and he and his fellow officers have been bloodied many times in their struggle to maintain peace. This officer is most adamant about surviving in this world and, as you will read, his mindset is so powerful that he will never give up. We have cleaned up the language a little.

In my mind, I'm never going to die in the street. Absolutely never. If a man tries to punch me in the head, the fight is on. If he cuts me, the fight is on. If I'm shot, the fight is on. I'm not losing a fight to a scumbag out there in the street. Period. That's it. No !%&*! out there is going to get me. The only way he gets me is to cut my head off, and I mean that. I'll fight you as long as I have breath left in me. I don't think any of those animals in that street can beat me. I've gone that way for 18 years patrolling those streets, and that's the way I'm going to keep on going. In my mind, you don't lose the fight.

If you were to ask this officer if he was afraid, he would tell you that he is. He would say that he doesn't try to be fearless, as that is impossible and a waste of energy. Instead, he uses his fear to fight back with such ferocity that he becomes—fearsome.

Tombstone courage

Using your fear for energy and ferocity does not mean that you forgo commonsense. Tombstone courage is foolish courage that results in injury or death. You have been training hard on your physical techniques and your mental imagery, which have given you tremendous skill and self-confidence. But—BUT—don't let that make you instigate a situation or wade into danger.

Your first objective when facing an attacker is always to get away, to take that avenue of escape, whether it's fleeing down a sidewalk or locking yourself in a bathroom.

Fighting back is always a last resort: The attacker is in front of you. He cannot be deterred. You cannot get away. You're scared but you're focused.

It's time to feed the lioness.

Use indignation as fuel

This technique relates to the last one, "Focus on the attack." It's different enough to stand alone but similar enough that they can be combined.

Loren knew a female police officer who quit after only a few months on the job because, as she said, "I just cannot accept that there are people out there who don't know me, but who are willing to hurt or kill me." She said that her life prior to being hired had been sheltered, one that focused on academia. The PD tried to help her develop the right mindset but in the end, she wanted out. She went on to be successful in another career.

It's indeed hard to accept that a person you don't know will hurt you without conscience to get your car, your money, your child, or to satisfy some sick need. It's also hard to accept that your partner, with whom you have trusted and shared so much of yourself, wants to degrade, hurt or even kill you.

Use this feeling, whether it's indignation, shock, outrage, fear, or anger, to charge your body and all your weapons with power and speed to attack back. *How dare you try to hurt me! I am a wife, a partner, a mother, a person who matters. You will not hurt me! I will hurt you! I will attack you with all my being!*

In the movie *Billy Jack*, an iconic independent film made 1971, Tom Laughlin, who plays a former Vietnam Green Beret and martial artist, walks into a café where three white men have just poured white flower over the heads of three Indian children. Billy Jack says through gritted teeth:

"When Jean and the kids at the school tell me that I'm supposed to control my violent temper, and be passive and nonviolent like they are, I try. I really try. Though when I see this girl... of such a beautiful spirit... so degraded... and this boy... that I love... sprawled out by this big ape here... and this little girl, who is so special to us we call her "God's little gift of sunshine"... and I think of the number of years that she's going to have to carry in her memory... the savagery of this idiotic moment of yours... I. Just. Go. BERSERK!"

Then Billy commences to beat the dog doo doo out of all three, demonstrating perfectly the use of indignation as fuel.

Think about this ahead of time. Think about how wrong it is, how insulting, how indignant, how enraging it is that someone wants to hurt what is dear to you. Use that feeling as fuel—rocket fuel.

Trigger

We discussed trigger words in Chapter Three, "the least you need to know," so we will just touch on it here. A trigger word is a blasting cap that ignites your physical techniques. When the creep grabs your arm, you scream, "Leave me alone!" or "No!" as you hit and kick him. Scream those words like an insane banshee each time you slam him with your best shots.

Trigger words can confuse an attacker, especially when you're hitting at the same time. Since the human brain can think of only one thing at a time, your piercing shouts and hammering weapons make it impossible for him to decide what to do, besides moving backwards and trying to cover up.

Trigger words:

- focus your mind.
- increase your power.
- turn your fear into energy.
- tell the attacker what you want.
- inform witnesses what is happening.

Some women choose curse words, and that is okay. What word(s) work for you?

Confidence

When you're confident, you have a bearing that tells attackers: "Don't mess with me." You're cool and self-assured because you're prepared for anything that comes your way. Confidence is a byproduct of:

- understanding fear.
- hard physical training.
- physical fitness.
- knowledge of environmental weapons.
- employing the four color zones.
- developing alertness and awareness skills.
- knowing at what point you will act physically.
- thinking and practicing safety everyday.
- knowing the laws where you live.

While fear is a complex issue that is the subject of countless books, articles and blogs, the simple techniques presented in this text have helped students understand it and use it to their benefit. See the resources section at the back of this book for additional reading.

How important is training with a padded opponent?

Classes should incorporate real life situations to work on, using uncomplicated techniques, and fighting hard with an attacker wearing padding.

■ ■ ■

One teaching technique I like applies to the principle that a woman will often be more protective of others than she is of herself. When using padded suit training, create scenarios where women are protecting someone else and watch what happens.

■ ■ ■

Women need to be taught the effects of adrenal stress. Students need to understand that when they are under extreme duress, certain physical changes manifest themselves in the body; i.e. shallow breathing, increased heart rate, fight or flight response, etc., and that proper training, especially against a padded attacker, will teach them how to use these instinctive responses as an aid rather than a hindrance.

■ ■ ■

I try to bring a feeling of empowerment to the participants in my classes. "You may be attacking me, but you WILL regret it, and I will NOT go down without a hell of a fight."

■ ■ ■

I have been to workshops where they use a "woofer," someone who deliberately antagonizes you to get your adrenal stress levels to rise. I found them to be very effective, but I also left with the words still ringing in my head. They were extremely upsetting and even though I know that it was just an exercise, that fear, anger, and rage is what I remembered most from the experience.

■ ■ ■

In working with women who have been battered or otherwise victimized, I teach them to say to themselves: "I am worth fighting for, I deserve to live a long and happy life," or whatever else helps them to get through an attack. It gives their minds something to focus on, and sets the scene, if you will, for their responses. Practice this when attacking a padded threat.

CHAPTER THIRTEEN

REALITY-BASED TRAINING

Authors' Note: FAST Defense is one of the most experienced *of all reality-based training programs in existence. Bill Kipp, founder of the worldwide organization, has personally endorsed every professional instructor that has trained and empowered thousands of women to control and function in the adrenal stress response that can occur in a verbal and physical confrontation. FAST Defense is recognized globally as an elite organization that gets results, well, fast. The prestigious magazine Black Belt recently named FAST Defense as the "Best Women's Program." In Bill's words:*

The world of women's self-defense has come a long way over the years. No longer the exclusive domain of burly ex-cops teaching fancy wristlocks and throws, today's discerning women are privy to the same advanced scenario-based training previously available only to elite SWAT and military units. Such an evolution has proven positive not only for the women who have benefited from the training but also for the science of reality self-defense training in general. By bringing scenario training out of the "top secret" closet, much has been learned and improved upon through literally hundreds of thousands of live scenarios to see what people can be trained to do in real situations.

In reality-based training, you learn to use fear as fuel.

UNDERSTANDING WHAT REALITY TRAINING IS AND IS NOT

Reality-based training has experienced a surge in popularity among the self-defense and martial arts industries. Yet much confusion still exists around it, which in some cases has caused more damage than good. Reality training is not necessarily about recreating a brutally real situation for the students to face and overcome. That would be akin to sending students out to the dark alleys to learn to protect themselves. They might survive the experience, but more often than not, it is going to go wrong.

Sadly, stories abound of well-meaning instructors unwittingly revictimizing a trusting student by putting them back into situations in which they previously failed, such as making a woman who has been carjacked get back in her car and recreate the incident. The motivation behind this approach is usually to help rewrite a new ending to the old story and reverse the feeling of victimization by giving them success. However, this method is a razor's edge, with a real danger of retraumatizing the person if things don't go to plan. When done correctly, scenario-based training can work miracles. But when done incorrectly, it can be like putting gas on a fire; it can cause serious emotional harm to the student.

With just a few exceptions, the theme for reality training is to set up the student for success. (right photo, Bill Kipp in the background.)

Our adage is this: We do as we train. If we train to fail, we are likely to fail under pressure. Conversely, if we train to win, a successful outcome is much more likely. Thus, the purpose of a scenario is to get the student to successfully learn and apply a particular set of skills or techniques under varying levels of pressure. Scenarios should start with low levels of intensity to set the student up for success, with successive scenarios building on the previous success to imprint positive action modes in a safe and predictable manner. This reality springboard has proven to provide students of all abilities high levels of proficiency in a relatively short time.

ASYMMETRIC VS. SYMMETRIC TRAINING

The concept is simple: Just as someone can be conditioned to freeze by a single short traumatic event in their childhood, one that can stay with them for years or decades, we can condition positive responses and action modes in a short time. Most self-defense training is done symmetrically, such as two people agreeing to spar one another. Yet real attacks occur asymmetrically, meaning the attacker is prepared but the defender is not. Real attacks are not a mutually agreed upon event. This is why most symmetrical training fails in the heat of battle. The solution is asymmetrical scenario-based training in which the student is set up for success. Although simple in concept, it does require skill to accomplish. But when done correctly, the results can be astounding.

Students discover an internal strength they never knew possible.

THE POWER OF VOICE

By far the most important self-defense skill set for women is to overcome verbal intimidation that most predators use effectively against their victims. Verbal defense scenarios are the toughest skill sets to teach and to learn, yet they are the skills that allow most women to stop an attack before it turns physical. Should that not work, students learn simple, high-percentage techniques to vulnerable areas on the attacker's body, and to fight back with all the fury they can muster. Success stories pour in from students who have effectively used these skills acquired after just hours of this unique asymmetrical training method.

Heavy padding (left) allows you to hit and kick the "attacker" full force.

Arguably, no other organization in the world has more experience teaching reality-based scenario training than FAST Defense. With an international network of instructors who come from a wide variety of martial arts and law enforcement backgrounds, FAST Defense instructors have honed scenario training to a fine science. Each instructor has been personally trained by Bill Kipp, FAST Defense founder, and former US Marine Recon Team Leader. Collectively, they have logged hundreds of thousands of live reality scenarios with children, teens, women, and men, learning empirically what works and what does not. Their success stories speak volumes that scenario based training is here to stay.

www.fastdefense, bill@fastdefense.com, 720-256-3898

Resources

National Domestic Violence Hotline at 1-800-799-7233

Why Does He Do That?: Inside the Minds of Angry and Controlling Men, Lundy Bancroft, Berkley Trade, ISBN-13: 978-0425191651

How to Spot a Dangerous Man Before You Get Involved, M. A. Sandra L. Brown, Hunter House, ISBN-10: 0897934474

Safe in the City, Marc MacYoung, Paladin Press, ISBN-10: 0873647750

Fear Less, Gavin de Becker, Little, Brown and Company, ISBN-10: 0316085960

The Gift of Fear, Gavin de Becker, Dell, ISBN-10: 0440508835

Warriors, Loren W. Christensen, Paladin Press, ISBN-10: 1581606966

On Combat, Lt. Col. Dave Grossman, Loren W. Christensen, Warrior Science Publications, ISBN-10: 0964920549

Fighting the Pain Resistant Attacker, Loren W. Christensen, Turtle Press, ISBN-10: 1934903183

Solo Training, Loren W. Christensen, Turtle Press, ISBN-10: 1880336596

Verbal Judo, Dr. George Thompson, Harper Paperbacks, ISBN-10: 0060577657

The Fighter's Body, Wim Demmere and Loren W. Christensen, Turtle Press, ISBN-10: 1880336812

Warrior Mindset, Dr. Mike Askens, Loren W. Christensen, Lt. Col. Dave Grossman, Warrior Science Publications, ISBN-10: 0964920557

Vital Targets : A Street-Savvy Guide to Targeting the Eyes, Ears, Nose, and Throat, DVD, Loren Christensen, Paladin Press, ASIN: B000H5NM0S

The Brutal Art of Ripping, Poking, and Pressing Vital Targets, DVD, Loren W. Christensen, Paladin Press, ASIN: B0030W1PLI

Solo Training, DVD, Loren W. Christensen, Turtle Press, ASIN: B000BBYSOM

Trauma and Recovery: The Aftermath of Violence--from Domestic Abuse to Political Terror, Judith Herman, Basic Books, ISBN: 978-0465087303

Photo by A'lyse Place

About the Authors

Lisa A. Place began training in the martial arts in the mid 1990s, earning belts in taekwondo, kempo, American freestyle, kickboxing, jujitsu and arnis. She has extensive teaching experience in the martial arts working with adults and children.

Lisa began training with Loren in 2003, and has appeared in several of his books and DVDs. She has been the principal photographer for numerous martial arts books and magazine articles.

Lisa can be contacted through her website: www.lisaplacebeadzone.com

Loren W. Christensen began training in the martial arts in 1965 and continues to this day. Over the years, he has earned a total of 11 black belts, eight in karate, two in jujitsu and one in arnis. Because of his nearly three decades in law enforcement, Loren's focus in the martial arts—writing, teaching and training —has always been on street survival, not competition.

Loren began his law enforcement career in 1967 as a Military Policeman in the Army and then joined the Portland (Oregon) Police Bureau an 1972, retiring in 1997. During his years on PPB, he worked street patrol, child abuse investigation, dignitary protection, Intelligence, street gangs, and as a defensive tactics instructor.

As a professional writer since 1978, Loren has penned over 45 published books with five publishers, dozens of magazine articles, and edited a police newspaper for nearly eight years. He has written on the martial arts, missing children, street gangs, school shootings, workplace violence, police-involved shootings, nutrition, exercise, prostitution, and various street subcultures. Loren has starred in seven martial arts training videos. From 2007 through 2008, Loren was included in the *Heritage Registry of Who's Who* for his accomplishments in publishing.

Loren can be contacted through his website LWC Books at www.lwcbooks.com

Index

poking 46
positioning 19–20
posture 21, 27
power 77, 78, 90, 203
practice 31, 134–148
preemptive hitting 158, 166
proactive 17
proximity 193
punch 38, 46, 54
push 24, 43, 83
pushups 121–124, 132, 141

R

rage 152–153
raking 46, 49, 107
range 159–160
rape 15, 23, 114
reality-based training 205–207
rear elbow 57, 107
rear-leg round knee 94
rear straight knee 91
rear wrist grab 117
red zone 16
reps 130, 131, 137
resources 21, 46, 146, 209
respect 29
response preparation 172
rest breaks 139
ribs 94
road rage 193–194
round knee strike 92–94
rules of engagement 196
running 165, 192

S

scenarios 105–118
script 114
self-defense 14, 34, 76, 77, 78, 84, 86, 118, 140–141,
    148, 170, 190
self-esteem 26
serial killing 15
sets 137
settings 141
shield block 108, 111, 165, 190
shin kick 20, 70, 72–75, 109, 114, 116, 117, 139,
    147, 160, 166
shin kick to groin 136
shirt grab 116
shredding 46–48
side elbow 59, 106
side hammerfist 106
side-handled baton 35
side plank 127–128

side stomp kick 62–67, 107, 117, 136, 139, 145, 147,
    187
signals 19
simplicity 34
situational awareness 150, 170
slap 24, 79–81, 112, 138, 139, 189, 190
slow motion mental imagery 180
soft target 82
solar plexus 65, 94
speed 78, 138
spouse 23
squats 129–131, 132, 141
stages of an attack 16
stalker 23
Stalking Resource Center 23
stance 27–28
static position 63
statistics 23
step back 65
stepping 36–37, 62
stomp 86–89, 117, 138, 139, 144, 160, 163
straight baton 35
straight knee strike 91–93
stranger 11, 15–20, 151, 188
strength 118, 121, 196
stress 166
submission 10–11
surprise 19, 172
surrounded 20
sweating 155

T

targets 17, 40, 116, 188, 190
techniques 32–35, 75–78
threat 20, 27, 29, 151, 193
threatening 22, 30, 154–155
thrusting 50, 82
tone of voice 29
touching 19, 25
training 184–185
training aerobically 137, 139
training frequency 134
trigger words 60, 202–203

U

uneven pushups 124
upward elbow 57
U.S. Department of Justice 23

V

Verbal Judo 30
vertical blow 41
vertical hammerfist 44, 135

vertical hammerfist strike 39
victim 11, 23, 25, 114, 158, 169
violent crime 23
vision loss 50
voice 29
voice tone 21

W

wall pushups 122
weapon 17, 28, 64, 96–103, 151, 158–159, 159,
     188, 192, 194
weight 41, 86
what-if questions 199–200
when-then sentences 200
white zone 16, 19
windshield wiper raking 49
words 30–31
workouts 120, 132, 139–141
wrist grab 117

Y

yellow zone 16, 17, 18, 19, 22, 25, 167, 200

Other Self-defense Books from Turtle Press:

Fighting the Pain Resistant Attacker
Total Defense
Kung Fu Grappling
Street Stoppers
Vital Point Strikes
Defensive Tactics
Secrets of Unarmed Gun Defenses
Point Blank Gun Defenses
Security Operations
Fighter's Fact Book 2
The Science of Takedowns, Throws and Grappling for Self-defense
Fighting Science
Solo Training
Solo Training 2
Fighter's Fact Book
Conceptual Self-defense
Combat Strategy
Taekwondo Self-defense

For more information:
Turtle Press
1-800-778-8785
e-mail: orders@turtlepress.com

http://www.turtlepress.com